CYNGOR CAERDYDD
CARDIFF COUNCIL
LIBRARY SERVICE

CARDIFF
CAERDYDD

1 1 MAR 2008		
1 3 DEC 2008		
- 3 FEB 2005		
2 6 FEB 2005		
1 1 MAR 2005		
0 2 JUN 2005		
0 6 OCT 2005		2:4:14
2 4 JAN 2006		
1 3 FEB 2006		
3 0 MAR 2006		
1 4 MAY 2007		

This book must be returned or renewed on or before the
latest date above, otherwise a fine will be charged.
Rhaid dychwelyd neu adnewyddu y llyfr hwn erbyn y dyddiad
diweddaraf uchod, neu bydd dirwy i'w thalu.

19Sg/54   LAB01

The Power of the
CASTLES

The Power of the
CASTLES

R. C. Riley & Peter Waller

OPC

An imprint of
Ian Allan Publishing

625.261
RIL

Contents

Half title:
A classic view of trains departing from Paddington: on 16 April 1957 No 5095 *Barbury Castle* passes under Westbourne Bridge with a down express. *R. C. Riley*

Title page:
Shortly before the outbreak of World War 2, No 5010 *Restormel Castle* heads eastbound through Patchway with the 12.30pm service from Newport to Paddington. *R. C. Riley collection*

First published 2003

ISBN 0 86093 587 6

© Ian Allan Publishing 2003

Published by Oxford Publishing Co

an imprint of Ian Allan Publishing Ltd, Hersham, Surrey KT12 4RG.

Printed by Ian Allan Printing Ltd, Hersham, Surrey KT12 4RG.

Code: 0310/B

Introduction

The 'Power of' volumes have, over the years, been one of the most enduring of all the series produced by OPC under its varying ownership. One of the most curious aspects of the series, however, was that, despite the obvious bias of OPC towards the GWR and BR(WR), no single class of Great Western Railway locomotive had been featured. In starting to rectify this omission, there can be no better choice than the classic 'Castle' class of 4-6-0 designed by Charles Benjamin Collett OBE.

Collett was born in 1871 and was trained from the start for a career in engineering, initially with the marine engineers Maudslay, Sons & Field Ltd of London. In 1893 he moved to Swindon as a draughtsman and, demonstrating obvious aptitude for his chosen career, he rose rapidly through the hierarchy at Swindon: assistant to the Chief Draughtsman in 1898; Assistant Works Manager in June 1900; Works Manager in December 1912; and Deputy Chief Mechanical Engineer in May 1919. He was, therefore, aged just over 50, the obvious candidate to succeed Churchward when the latter retired at the end of 1921. Collett took over the reins at Swindon on 1 January 1922, the start of a role that was to last almost 20 years, until his retirement in June 1941 aged 70. Collett was to die, aged 81, on 23 August 1952.

Under Collett's administration, the policy of standardisation, pioneered by his predecessor, was maintained, as the company concentrated upon interchangeability of boilers and the production of large numbers of locomotives within a relatively small number of classes. There were distinct advantages to the railway of this policy, in terms of reduced running costs and ease of maintenance. In his 20 years at the helm, Collett produced 13 different classes of steam locomotive, including five different classes of 4-6-0: the 'Castles' of 1923, the 'Halls' of 1924, the 'Kings' of 1927, the 'Granges' of 1936 and the 'Manors' of 1938. In total, more than 550 4-6-0 locomotives to Collett's designs were constructed over the near 30-year period.

The first of Collett's classic designs to emerge was the 'Castle' class, with the first, No 4073 *Caerphilly Castle*, unveiled at Paddington station on 23 August 1923, barely 20 months after his appointment. The locomotive, a development of Churchward's 'Star' class of 1907, was 10% more powerful than the earlier class and was to prove, against competition with Gresley's new Pacifics for the GNR — both theoretical and later practical — to be the most powerful passenger locomotives then in service on any railway in Britain. The 10% gain in power was gained by increasing the width of the cylinders by one inch to 16in and by adopting a larger boiler. Retaining the 225lb/sq in boiler pressure, the new design gave a tractive effort of 31,625lb at 85%, which was considerably greater than the 27,800lb of the earlier class. In theory, the original concept for the class would have resulted in an even more powerful

Above:
On 21 June 1955 No 7004 *Eastnor Castle* is seen at
Swindon at the head of the down 'South Wales Pullman'.
Brian Morrison

locomotive, as the initial scheme had envisaged use of the
larger No 7 boiler used on the '47xx' class. However, the
need to keep the class within the 20ton axle load restriction
resulted in the use of a smaller No 8 boiler.

The first 10 of the class were constructed between August
1923 and April 1924 and, during 1924, the prototype was
to be displayed within the Palace of Engineering at the
British Empire Exhibition at Wembley close to Sir Nigel
Gresley's Pacific *Flying Scotsman*. The GWR proudly
proclaimed its locomotive to be the most powerful
passenger locomotive in Britain and, between 29 April and
4 May 1925, the competing claims were put to the test,
with No 4079 *Pendennis Castle* being put to work on
services between London and Grantham or Doncaster
alongside LNER Pacifics Nos 4475 *Flying Fox* and 2545
Silver Jubilee, whilst, on the GWR main line, LNER Pacific
No 4474 *Victor Wild* operated on the 'Cornish Riviera
Express' in competition with No 4074 *Caldicot Castle*. Both
Gresley's and Collett's designs performed well, although it
was the latter's that ultimately took the honours in terms of

fuel economy and acceleration, with the result that Gresley
modified the specifications of his Pacifics.

The competition with the LNER Pacifics was not the
only occasion when Collett's design proved superior to
those of other companies. In 1926, the LMSR borrowed
No 5000 *Launceston Castle* for trials on the West Coast
main line. The LMS was faced by an hiatus over the
provision of motive power for the route; Fowler was
planning a class of Pacifics — ultimately never built — and
the earlier generation of express locomotives, such as the
'Claughtons', were no longer adequate. The performance of
the 'Castle' on LMS metals was such as to encourage the
board to enquire about ordering 50 from Swindon or,
alternatively, to allow Derby to build them under license.
However, the GWR was reluctant and, combined with
problems over the loading gauge, this resulted in the idea
not being progressed. However, the result of the experiment
was the construction of the 'Royal Scot' class to a design by
Fowler.

Following the construction of the first 10 of the class, the
11th was to emerge in September 1924. This was No 111
Viscount Churchill which was, in fact, a rebuild of the
GWR's only Pacific, Churchward's *The Great Bear* of 1908.
The locomotive was renamed after the then chairman of
the GWR. The conversion, however, was not without
controversy as it had been undertaken without the sanction
of the GWR's board. The locomotive, which had been the

Above:
No 7026 *Tenby Castle* heads into London on 4 May 1957
with an up football excursion at Northolt junction.
R. C. Riley

first Pacific constructed for use on a railway in Britain, had
been regarded as prestigious and Collett's unauthorised
modification resulted in him being censured. In operational
terms, however, he was correct; the Pacific was highly route
limited, its unique No 6 boiler needed extensive repairs
(including a new inner firebox) and it also required a major
overhaul. One beneficial consequence, however, of the
contentious conversion was that Sir Felix Pole, the then
General Manager, was made aware of the 20ton axle
loading and when larger locomotives were required three
years later — the 'Kings' being the result — he demanded
that the axle loading for specific routes be increased to
22.5ton (a standard which, ironically, the Civil Engineering
Department was already adhering to). No 111 was one of
16 earlier locomotives to be rebuilt as members of the
'Castle' class between 1924 and 1940.

Apart from the rebuilt locomotives, production of new
locomotives continued in batches of 10 per annum: Nos
4083-4092 between May and August 1925; Nos 4093-99,
5000-2 between May and September 1926; and Nos 5003-
12 between May and July 1927. There was then a five-year
gap before production recommenced with No 5013 in June
1932. Ten locomotives, Nos 5013-22, were constructed
that year, to be followed by a further 10 (Nos 5023-32),

in 1934 and a similar number (Nos 5033-42) in 1935. The
following year was to see 15 new locomotives constructed,
Nos 5043-57, 10 more in 1937 (Nos 5058-67), 10 in 1938
(Nos 5068-77) and 10 in 1939 (Nos 5078-82/93-7). The
first new locomotive to emerge following the cessation of
hostilities was No 5098 in May 1946 and a total of 10 —
Nos 5098/9, 7000-7 — were completed that year; No 7007,
appropriately renamed *Great Western*, was the last of the
class to be constructed under GWR ownership. A further
batch of 10 locomotives, Nos 7008-17, was constructed in
1948, 10 (Nos 7018-27) in 1949 and a final batch of 10
(Nos 7028-37) in 1950. The postwar construction was
probably necessitated by the need to replace the life-expired
'Star' class locomotives that would have been withdrawn
much earlier save for the exigencies of World War 2. The
last to be constructed, No 7037, was named *Swindon* by
HRH Princess Elizabeth in honour of its birthplace on
15 November 1950. During the 40-year career of the class,

there were inevitably developments in construction, detail and modification. These are discussed more fully in the section entitled 'Variations on a Theme' (see pp14-20). Of these improvements the most significant were perhaps the last: the fitting of double chimneys, double blast pipe and a four-row superheater boiler. These improved the class's steaming and performance significantly, although not all the class was treated, and undoubtedly led to the type surviving longer.

The initial allocation of the class was to Old Oak Common, Laira and Newton Abbot sheds, with the locomotives operating primarily upon express services to and from the West Country. Almost from the start the class proved itself to be highly successful, success born out by trials with No 4074 and the dynamometer in 1924, which showed a remarkably low coal consumption — 2.83lb/drawbar hp (at a time when the norm was between 4lb and 5lb) — resulting in a saving in coal consumption over the

'Stars' of some 6-7%. As the numbers of the class increased so the list of routes over which they operated increased, with the type ultimately seeing service on most of the GWR's Class One services. The introduction of the more powerful 'King' class saw the newer type allocated to many of the GWR's most prestigious services; however, 'Castles' could substitute for 'Kings' and did so on a regular basis, although their lower power output meant that they always struggled to keep to 'King' class schedules.

The first members of the class were attached to the then-standard 3,500gal tender; in 1927, Collett designed a new 4,000gal tender — later modified to include a welded tank used on Nos 5098/99 and 7000-2 — and this became the standard tender for the class — with the exception of the unique eight-wheel tender — until the construction of the Hawksworth straight-sided tender fitted initially to Nos 7008-37. Inevitably, however, as tenders were inter-changeable it became possible to see earlier locomotives with Hawksworth tenders and later examples with the standard 4,000gal type.

As the class's numbers increased, so the class came to allocated to many of the GWR's main locomotive sheds, including Wolverhampton Stafford Road, Cardiff Canton and Bristol Bath Road. One of the services with which the class came to be closely associated was the 'Cheltenham Flyer' and, such was the prowess of the class on this service that, on 6 June 1932 No 5006 *Tregenna Castle* achieved the 77.3 miles from Swindon to Paddington in just under 57min at an average speed of some 81.7mph.

By the 1930s, the construction of the 'Castle' class along with other more modern designs by Collett had resulted in the rapid elimination of older express locomotive classes. The casualties during this period included various types of Dean-designed 4-4-0s, including the 'Bulldog' and 'Duke' classes, and, in mid-1937, it was decided to transfer the names of some of these locomotives (supplemented by additional names) to recently-constructed members of the 'Castle' class. The first to be so treated was No 5063 *Thornbury Castle* which became *Earl Baldwin*, name after the recently retired Conservative Prime Minister (who had been granted the hereditary title Earl Baldwin of Bewdley on his retirement), in July 1937. This was destined not to be the only occasion on which a significant number of the class were to be renamed as a result of circumstances; during World War 2 a number of the class were renamed after aircraft associated with the Royal Air Force and the Fleet Air Arm.

The last of the rebuilt locomotives, converted from 'Star' class 4-6-0s were constructed between April 1937 and November 1940; the last two — Nos 5087 (in November 1940) and 5089 (in October 1939) — were in fact the only members of the class constructed during the period of hostilities. The 10 rebuilt 'Stars' were not amongst the most successful of the class as the lengthened frames proved prone to cracking.

By the cessation of hostilities in 1945, Collett had retired, being replaced by Hawksworth, but production of the class resumed in May 1946 and was to continue through to August 1950, by which time the GWR had been subsumed into the newly-nationalised British Railways. Contemporaneously with the construction of the last of the class, the first withdrawals occurred, with No 4009 being withdrawn in March 1950, to be followed closely by three more of the early rebuilds — Nos 111, 4016 and 4032 — but it was not until the late 1950s that further withdrawals commenced as Western Region introduced the new classes of diesel-hydraulic locomotive into services. Wholesale withdrawals, however, did not make serious inroads into the class until 1960. Such was the pace of the transition from steam, that by the end of 1963 only 51 remained in service and, 12 months later, this number had been further reduced to 13.

The last scheduled departure of a 'Castle'-hauled service from Paddington occurred on 13 April 1965 when No 7022 *Hereford Castle* hauled the 4.15pm stopping service to Banbury via Bicester; the locomotive, bereft of nameplates and without its correct number plate presented a sorry sight. However, the WR made up for this on 11 June 1965, when the official last steam-hauled service from Paddington (again the 4.15pm service to Banbury), was hauled by No 7029 *Clun Castle* with a suitable headboard and with its GWR number reinstated on its buffer beam.

The last two of the class in service, Nos 7029/30, were officially withdrawn in December 1965, although the former, by this time preserved, was to appear occasionally on freight services on the Birmingham-Oxford line during early 1966. By the time that the class was being withdrawn, regional reorganisation had resulted in some being transferred to the London Midland Region and, with the closure of the ex-GWR shed at Stafford Road in Wolverhampton, being allocated to such non-GWR sheds as Oxley.

Following withdrawal, No 4073 made a remarkable journey by road to the Science Museum in South Kensington, where it was to form a central part of the museum's display for almost four decades, until a change of policy saw it transferred to the National Railway Museum at York. Also to be preserved on withdrawal were Nos 4079 and 7029. No 4079 can perhaps claim to be the most widely travelled representative of the class, having been operational in Australia for a number of years prior to its repatriation. A number of other representatives of the class were sold initially to the famous scrapyard of Woodham Bros at Barry in South Wales; these examples, Nos 5029 (rescued in May 1976), 5043 (August 1973), 5051 (February 1970), 5080 (August 1974) and 7027 (August 1972), ensure that no fewer than eight of Collett's classic design have survived into the 21st century.

Acknowledgements

A book of this nature cannot be compiled without the assistance of the many photographers whose work is represented, some of whom unfortunately are no longer with us. We would like to thank all those whose work appears herein and those who have helped us with photographs: Julian Peters, Barry Hoper, Norman Preedy, the National Railway Museum and in particular, Barry Hayward for his assistance with the photographs taken by the late Kenneth Leech. Over the years, the 'Castle' class has featured in countless books and magazine articles, and researchers seeking further information on the class can obtain this from these titles, amongst many others:

'Castles' and 'Kings' at Work; Michael Rutherford; Ian Allan
    Publishing 1982
Collett & Hawksworth Locomotives; Brian Haresnape;
    Ian Allan Publishing 1978
Great Western 4-6-0s; Brian Stephenson; Ian Allan
    Publishing 1984
Portraits of the 'Castles'; Bryan Holden and Kenneth Leech;
    Moorland 1981
Steam in Action: 'Castles'; Laurence Waters; Ian Allan
    Publishing 1991
The GWR Stars, Castles and Kings Part 2 1930-1965;
    O. S. Nock; David & Charles 1970
*The Locomotives of the GWR Part 8: Modern Passenger
    Classes*; RCTS 1953
*What Happened to Steam: Vol 2 The Great Western Castles
    and Kings*; P. B. Hands 1980

Above:

The first of the 'Castle' class to emerge, in August 1923 (only 20 months after Collett's appointment) was No 4073 *Caerphilly Castle.* As was traditional, the locomotive was recorded for an official photograph in grey, a livery which serves well to indicate a number of the features of the early members of the class. Note the narrow outside steam pipes and diagonal rain strip on the cab roof.

Another feature evident in the photograph is the provision of bogie brakes; these were fitted to the first 10 members of the class alone and were later removed. The 'Castle' class differed from the early 'Star' class most obviously in look by the extension to the cab and the provision of cab-side windows. A standard 3,500gal tender was fitted when new. *Ian Allan Library*

Right:

In 1924 an exhibition was held at Wembley to celebrate the British Empire. One of the displays was called the 'Palace of Engineering' and one exhibit in that display was the then-new No 4073, which had been repainted in a special livery for the event. This view, taken in November 1924, shows the locomotive being removed from the exhibition. In order to return the engines displayed at Wembley to the main line, part of the wall of the display hall had to be demolished. *R. C. Riley Collection*

Above:
As part of its display at the 1924 Empire Exhibition, the GWR had claimed that the 'Castle' represented Britain's most powerful passenger locomotive design. Close by was another contender for that title, Sir Nigel Gresley's No 4472 *Flying Scotsman*, and it was inevitable that the claim would be put to the test. Thus early the following year, No 4079 *Pendennis Castle* spent a week, 29 April to 4 May, based at King's Cross where it could be tested against Gresley's designs whilst another Gresley Pacific was sent to Old Oak Common to be tested against the GWR designs. Pictured at King's Cross shed during this period is the 'Castle' alongside one of the 'A1' Pacifics, No 4475 *Flying Fox*, against which the tests were made. *R. C. Riley Collection*

Left:
No 4079 *Pendennis Castle* is seen departing from King's Cross station during the week's trial on the LNER. Although both types performed well, it was the 'Castle' that excelled with superior acceleration and better fuel consumption. Based upon the experience of the tests, Gresley modified his designs to incorporate higher boiler pressure and longer valve travel. *R. C. Riley Collection*

Right:
Another unusual London terminus to witness a member of the 'Castle' class was Euston. No 5000 *Launceston Castle* worked over LMS metals for a short period in November 1926. For example, on 10 and 12 November it hauled the 10am Euston-Glasgow service between Crewe and Carlisle returning to Crewe on 11 and 13 November at the head of the 10am Glasgow-Euston train. The locomotive is seen at Euston having arrived at the head of an up express. The locomotive was returned to Old Oak Common, via the Willesden loop, on 20 November. Whilst the 'Castle' was being tested on the LMS, Midland 'Compound' 4-4-0 No 1047 was to be seen on the GWR between Paddington and Bristol. *Ian Allan Library*

Above:
On 21 April 1924 No 4079 *Pendennis Castle* heads westwards near Dawlish Warren with the down 'Cornish Riviera Express'.
H. G. W. Household/Courtesy National Railway Museum

Left:
No 4086 *Builth Castle* was built at Swindon in June 1925; the locomotive is seen at Exeter when barely a year old. *A. C. Roberts/ R. C. Riley Collection*

Below:
On 30 June 1925, No 4083 *Abbotsbury Castle* heads eastwards with the 10.25am Bristol-Swindon local at Chipping Sodbury troughs. The locomotive was constructed the previous month and so, presumably, this was a running in turn. The eclectic collection of coaching stock in the consist, including four- and six-wheel coaches as well as vans, is worthy of note. *H. G. W. Household/ Courtesy National Railway Museum*

Above:
No 4078 *Pembroke Castle* heads westwards at Twyford with a down excursion. *R. C. Riley Collection*

Below:
Pictured at Aller Junction in 1927, No 4009 *Shooting Star* heads west towards Penzance with the down 'Cornish Riviera' express. No 4009 would be renumbered and renamed 100A1 *Lloyd's* in January 1936. Aller Junction signalbox would survive for considerably longer, not being decommissioned until the late 1980s. *A. C. Cawston*

Above:

Inevitably, in a class that featured more than 160 locomotives constructed over a near 30-year period, there were variations and modifications. The original No 4082 *Windsor Castle* of April 1924, recorded at Swindon on 8 August 1928, illustrates many of the standard features of the class as constructed before World War 2. All the prewar locomotives built new and the rebuilt 'Stars', plus No 111 (the only Pacific locomotive, No 111 *The Great Bear* built for the GWR which was rebuilt as a 'Castle' in 1924), possessed boilers with two-row superheaters and sight feed lubricators. No 4082 also shows the tall chimney that was fitted to the class until 1936, the curved casing for the inside cylinders (as fitted to Nos 4073-5012), the inset frame at the front end (derived from the 'Star' class and designed to clear the leading bogie wheels, being fitted to Nos 4073-92 along with the 'Star' rebuilds) and the GWR-style taper buffers. *Ian Allan Library*

Variations on a Theme

Left:

No 4009 *Shooting Star* is seen in 1925 shortly after its conversion to the 'Castle' Class. This offside view illustrates well the tapered frame at the front end that was typical of the early members of the 'Castle' class as well as those rebuilt from the earlier 'Star' class. *R. C. Riley Collection*

Above:

No 5028 *Llantilio Castle* was built at Swindon in May 1934. This view from the nearside taken at Swindon Works shows to good effect the straight framing at the front that had become standard to the class with No 4093. Also clearly shown is the box pattern inside cylinder casing; this had become standard from No 5013 onwards. Finally, under the cab, can be seen the sanding gear; on all locomotives constructed up to No 5059 (and the 'Star' rebuilds), the sand box was located under the cab. *Ian Allan Library*

Above:

No 5012 *Berry Pomeroy Castle*, pictured at Old Oak Common in 1932, was the last of the class to be constructed new with the curved pattern cylinder casing. It was also fitted with the sand box located under the cab. *J. A. G. H. Coltas*

Left:
No 5092 *Tresco Abbey* is pictured at Bristol Bath Road on 6 April 1938. A 'Star' rebuild, the locomotive was fitted with the later pattern sand boxes, located externally. This modification was designed to make the sand boxes more accessible. The 'Star' rebuilds were never as successful as the locomotives built new, primarily as a result of a tendency to develop cracked frames where these had been extended. *R. C. Riley*

Above:
In 1931 the GWR constructed a single, experimental, eight-wheel tender (No 2586). This view shows the tender on 29 August 1936 when attached to No 5032 *Usk Castle*. This was the third locomotive to have been linked to the tender; in total 11 locomotives used it, seven of which were members of the 'Castle' class (Nos 4093, 5001/17/32/49/68/71). The tender was generally similar to the standard 4,000gal Collett design but weighed just over 49 tons when fully laden and was to survive until final withdrawal in November 1963. *Steamchest/R. C. Riley Collection*

Right:
The early 'Castles' were all fitted with a tall chimney; from 1936 onwards the new locomotives were constructed with a shorter chimney as shown by No 5053 *Earl Cairns* on 25 September 1948 as it heads towards Paddington with an up service from Birmingham at Ilmer Halt, near Princes Risborough. *J. F. Russell-Smith/Courtesy National Railway Museum*

Right:
Another view of No 5032 with its unique eight-wheel tender. This was the third locomotive to have operated with the tender, following on from 'Hall' Nos 5919 and 5001.
R. C. Riley Collection

Above:

In the 1930s, no doubt influenced by contemporary American practice, there was a fashion for streamlining. This was the era of Gresley's classic 'A4' design and of Stanier's Pacifics. Not to be left out, the GWR undertook the streamlining of two locomotives, a 'Castle' and a 'King'. The former was represented by eight-year-old No 5005 *Manorbier Castle*, which emerged so modified in March 1935. The locomotive is seen at Newton Abbot on 7 September 1935 whilst heading the 10.55am service from Paddington to Paignton. The experiment was not deemed successful and the streamlining was removed gradually over the next couple of years.
Rev John Goodman/R. C. Riley Collection

Left:

A total of five 'Castle' class locomotives — Nos 100A1, 5039/79/83/91 — were converted to oil-burning in 1946/47. Four of the five locomotives selected were fitted with the standard 4,000gal tender into which a fuel tank was added. The exception was No 5091, which operated with a 3,500gal tender. Another modification was the addition of sliding cab shutters on the outside of the cab windows. One of the quintet, No 5079 *Lysander* is pictured at Marazion on 25 August 1947 with the up 'Cornish Riviera Express'. All the oil-fired locomotives had reverted to coal by the end of 1948. *Rev A. C. Cawston*

Right:
Following the successful use of a double blastpipe and chimney on 'King' class No 6015 *King Richard III* in 1955, No 7018 *Drysllwyn Castle* was fitted with a double chimney in order to try and improve the locomotive's previously indifferent performance. On 13 May 1956, shortly after the locomotive was fitted with the double chimney, it was recorded outside Swindon Works. At this stage the locomotive still retained its three-row superheater boiler. The final major modification was to occur with the second of the class to be fitted with a double chimney, No 4090, which was also to be given a four-row superheater boiler. This view also shows well the modified outside steam pipe that was adopted as a replacement for the fracture-prone original straight design. *L. Nicolson*

Above:
The class was originally designed with the mechanical lubricator fitted behind the steam pipe, as shown in this view of No 5095 *Barbury Castle* at Cardiff Canton taken after the locomotive had been converted to double-chimney format in November 1958 and after its transfer to Shrewsbury in September 1960 (Shrewsbury was recoded to 89A in January 1961 and this photograph must date from between then and the locomotive's withdrawal in September 1962). *J. Hodge*

Left:
A number of the class saw the mechanical lubricator moved forward to the steam pipe. The reason for this change was to permit better access to the inside motion. The revised location of the lubricator is clearly shown in this view of No 4074 *Caldicot Castle* at Swindon shed on 13 August 1961. *P. J. Hurcum*

The Golden Age

Above:
Looking in superb excellent external condition, No 5001 *Llandovery Castle* waits at Leamington Spa station in 1931 with a down express service. *J. A. G. H. Coltas*

Below:
With the tide well in and few people on the sea wall, No 4093 *Dunster Castle*, built in May 1926, heads eastwards along the sea wall at Dawlish in 1932. *Ian Allan Library*

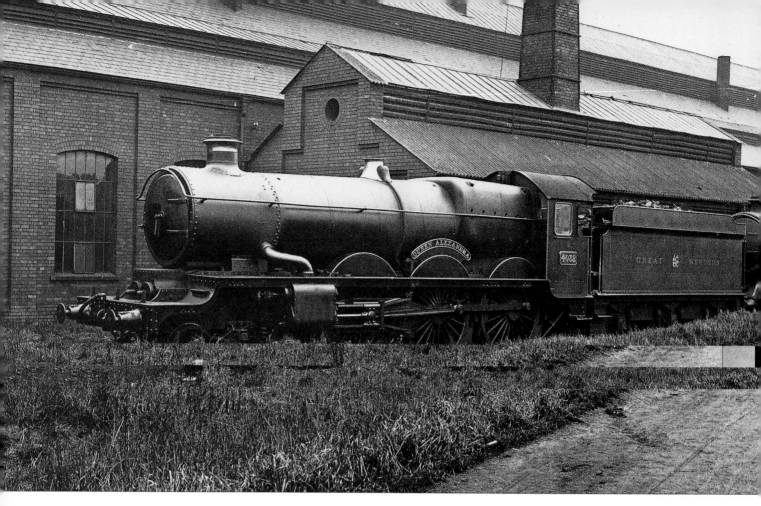

Left:
Pictured at Old Oak Common in 1932 is one of the 'Star' class 4-6-0s rebuilt as a 'Castle'. No 4032 *Queen Alexandra* was rebuilt in April 1926, the second of the 'Star' class to be so treated. *J. A. G. H. Coltas*

Below left:
Built in April 1936, No 5049 *Denbigh Castle* was less than a month old when recorded at Reading on a relief service from Bristol to Paddington. The locomotive was on loan from Swindon to Bath Road for running-in purposes. The locomotive would retain the name *Denbigh Castle* for only a short period, being renamed *Earl of Plymouth* in August 1937. *Ian Allan Library*

Above right:
'Star' class No 4009 *Shooting Star* had originally been converted into a 'Castle' class locomotive in April 1925. On 1 December 1935 the locomotive is pictured at Swindon shed shortly before entering the Works for overhaul. When the locomotive re-emerged in January 1936 it was as No 100A1 *Lloyd's*. Note the tall safety valve and 4,000gal tender. *H. F. Wheeller*

Below:
When the locomotive was first converted, it was simply numbered A1 and called *Lloyd's*. It is seen in this condition outside Swindon Works. *R. C. Riley Collection*

Left:
In 1936, in its new guise No 100A1 *Lloyd's* is seen at Leamington Spa station looking in superb external condition. *J. A. G. H. Coltas*

Right:
No 5050 *Devizes Castle* is seen at Swindon on 10 May 1936 in brand-new condition. The locomotive would bear this name for just over a year, being renamed *Earl of St Germans* in August 1937. *R. C. Riley Collection*

Centre right:
Heading an up service from Penzance eastwards at Wickwar Tunnel in 1936, No 5036 *Lyonshall Castle* was only a matter of months old when recorded, having been completed at Swindon in May 1935. *Ian Allan Library*

Below right:
Recorded at Westbury in 1936 at the head of a down service to Penzance, No 5029 *Nunney Castle* was at the time an Old Oak Common-allocated locomotive. *Ian Allan Library*

Left:
In 1935 Britain celebrated the Silver Jubilee of King George V; the happy year was, however, to be overshadowed early in the new year by the death of the monarch. On 28 January 1936, No 4082 *Windsor Castle* — the locomotive that the King had driven at Swindon more than a decade earlier — had the solemn task of heading the royal funeral train from Paddington to Windsor. All along the route, people stood by the trackside to pay their last respects to a popular monarch.
N. Shepherd/R. C. Riley Collection

Left:
A two-coach train formed of a non-corridor 'B' set was light work for No 4083 *Abbotsbury Castle* when photographed on a running-in turn on the up slow line at Bathampton in 1936. *Ian Allan Library*

Above:
No 5064 carried the name *Tretower Castle* for a relatively short period, from construction in June 1937 until it was renamed *Bishop's Castle* the following month. Given that the

locomotive in this view at Swindon carried the earlier name, it must date from that brief month-long period and therefore must record the locomotive when it was virtually brand new. *Ian Allan Library*

Above:
Albeit without a headboard, No 5003 *Lulworth Castle* is at the head of the 'Devonian' at Dawlish during the summer of 1936. *Ian Allan Library*

Right:
In 1938, No 4084 *Aberystwyth Castle* heads a down express near Brent Knoll. *Ian Allan Library*

Left:
When originally constructed in June 1938, No 5069 *Isambard Kingdom Brunel* was fitted with a non-standard nameplate as illustrated here.
D. B. Watkins/R. C. Riley Collection

Left:
The non-standard nameplates on No 5069 lasted only a relatively short period. When recorded at Leamington Spa station later in 1938, the nameplates had been replaced by those of the usual pattern. *J. A. G .H. Coltas*

Right:
Captured at speed near Hallavington in 1938, No 5037 *Monmouth Castle*, then only some three years old having been completed at Swindon in May 1935, powers an up service from South Wales. *Ian Allan Library*

Above:
Pictured at Swindon in 1938 is No 4016 *The Somerset Light Infantry (Prince Albert's)*. Converted from a 'Star' in October 1925, the locomotive had been named *Knight of the Golden Fleece* until early 1938. The locomotive was renamed in a ceremony held at Paddington station on 18 February 1938, with the new nameplates being unveiled by Gen Sir Walter Braithwaite, Colonel of the regiment. After the ceremony, No 4016 headed the 1.30pm West of England express out of Paddington. *Ian Allan Library*

Right:
In 1938, No 5036 *Lyonshall Castle* is seen passing Greenford on the 11.10am service from Paddington to Snow Hill. By this date, the threat of war with Germany was growing real but hostilities would not break out until September 1939. With the onset of war, the railway industry's priorities changed as the needs of the war economy took hold. The last wholly new prewar 'Castle' class locomotive, No 5097, emerged in June 1939, although it was not until November 1940 that the last of the 'Star' rebuilds was completed. There would be no further additions to the class until after World War 2 when No 5098 appeared in May 1946. *C. R. L Coles/ Rail Archive Stephenson*

'Castles' at War

Left:
It's September 1939 and the country, to recall Neville Chamberlain's words, 'is now at war with Germany'. The war, however, seems a million miles away from Penzance as No 5057 *Earl Waldegrave* backs its train from the station to the carriage sidings. The train's consist includes both GWR and LMS rolling stock. *B. A. Butt*

Centre left:
On 11 April 1940, during the period of the 'Phoney War', No 5081 *Penrice Castle* is seen at Cheltenham (Malvern Road). The locomotive shows clearly that the cab-side window has been plated over. This locomotive would retain its original name for only a relatively short period after the date of this photograph, being renamed *Lockheed Hudson* the following January. *L. B. Lapper/R. C. Riley Collection*

Below:
In 1940/41, a number of the class were renamed in tribute to aircraft flown by the Royal Air Force. The first to be so treated was No 5071, which was renamed after the Supermarine Spitfire in September 1940. Recorded in a photograph issued in August 1941, No 5071 is seen in its post-September 1940 condition with new nameplates. Note, also, the replacement of the glass in the cabside windows by metal and the eight-wheel tender (see pp.16, 17) No 5071 was the fourth locomotive to operate with the tender, following on from No 5032. *Ian Allan Library*

Above:

A close-up of the cab of No 4096 *Highclere Castle* taken at Swindon Works shows to good effect the modifications made to the cab for wartime operation. The cab-side window has been plated over — note, however, that the lining out has been carried over the plating — and an experimental (and impractical) screen installed to reduce the light from the fire during blackouts. *Ian Allan Library*

Below:

War in Europe ceased in May 1945 and that in the Far East three months later. Pictured on the 1.45pm service from Paddington to Stourbridge Junction, No 4086 *Builth Castle* passes Reading West Junction towards the end of the war. At this date, the locomotive still retains the plated-over cab-side windows, but these would be removed quickly once hostilities ceased. *Maurice Earley/Courtesy National Railway Museum*

Above:

At about 3am on 2 July 1941, No 4091 *Dudley Castle* was involved in a collision with LMS Class 8F No 8293 whilst at the head of the 6.20pm up service from Plymouth to Paddington. The '8F' was heading the 1.30am Old Oak Common-Severn Tunnel goods. The accident, which occurred at Dolphin Junction near Slough when the 'Castle' was crossing to the up relief line, resulted in the death of five passengers and many injured. One factor in the accident was the fact that, being on loan to the GWR, the '8F' was not fitted with ATC. The photograph shows the aftermath of the accident with the recovery of the two damaged locomotives in hand.
R. C. Riley Collection

Above:

After the cessation of hostilities, the control of the 'Big Four' reverted to the companies but there was a sense that all was about to change. A new Labour government, with an avowed policy of Nationalisation, had been elected with a large majority and the depredations of the wartime years had taken their toll on the nation's infrastructure.

Nationalisation of the railway industry was authorised by act in 1947 to take effect from 1 January 1948. Thus, when pictured here on 30 August 1947 at Slough with an up express, No 5020 *Trematon Castle* was to be a GWR locomotive for only a further four months. *J. F. Russell-Smith/ Courtesy National Railway Museum*

Left:

A further view from the autumn of the GWR's independent existence sees No 4000 *North Star* heading northwestwards over Ruislip troughs with the 4.10pm service from Paddington to Birmingham. The spray from beneath the tender confirms that the locomotive was taking water at this point. *C. R. L. Coles*

Right:

Whilst the newly Nationalised industry came into existence in 1948, for the travelling public it would take some time before the final vestiges of the old order disappeared; indeed, it could be argued that even today there remain enough traces of the 'Big Four' (and even their antecedents) to provide an object lesson in railway history. On 25 September 1948, No 5022 *Wigmore Castle* heads a down express at Ilmer Halt. To all intents and purposes, the scene could have been recorded a decade earlier; only the eagle eyed would have noticed the appearance of 'British Railways' on the locomotive's tender. *J. F. Russell-Smith/Courtesy National Railway Museum*

Left:

Before the newly-Nationalised railway industry settled on its new livery, a number of locomotives appeared in non-standard colours. One so treated was No 4091 *Dudley Castle*, which was briefly painted in a lined pea green livery, as shown here. The lining was in red and yellow. This livery was only carried for a short period before the locomotive reverted to the more traditional GWR dark green. *W. J. Reynolds*

Right:

One of the more obvious changes wrought by BR was the appearance of locomotive numberplates on the smokebox door. On 1 October 1949 No 5018 *St Mawes Castle*, heading an up local at Beaconsfield, bears this adornment, an undoubted boon to loco spotters, but otherwise remains in virtually original GWR condition (save for any indication of ownership on the tender). *J. F. Russell-Smith/ Courtesy National Railway Museum*

Left:
No **100A1** *Lloyd's* was one of the five locomotives converted to oil-burning immediately after World War 2. Pictured on 21 May 1948 at Old Oak Common, post-Nationalisation but still proclaiming its GWR antecedents, the locomotive shows well the modifications undertaken to convert the five to oil-burning, in particular the sliding shutter over the cab-side windows and the fuel tank in the standard 4,000gal tender. All the oil-fired locomotives were converted back to coal by the end of the year.
No 100A1 would be destined to become the first of the 'Castle' class to be withdrawn, succumbing in March 1950. *N. E. Preedy Collection*

Below:
On 13 April 1952 No **111** *Viscount Churchill* is seen near Uphill Junction with an up Sunday service from Plymouth to Paddington. By this date the Laira-allocated locomotive was coming towards the end of its long and illustrious career. It would be withdrawn in July 1953. The locomotive had originally been built as a Pacific in 1908 to a design by Churchward, named *The Great Bear*. Much to the consternation of his superiors, who had regarded the locomotive as one of the GWR's most prestigious, it had been rebuilt in September 1924, as the 11th member of the class. *J. D. Mills*

Right:
Pictured at Stratford upon Avon on 6 June 1952, No **4000** *North Star* was at this date allocated to Stafford Road. Historically one of the most important of the class, No 4000 had originally been built as an Atlantic in June 1906 and numbered 40. Experience with this and the GWR's other Atlantics convinced Churchward that the 4-6-0 was more suited to the company's needs and in 1907 the first of the 'Star' class emerged. In 1909 No 40, renumbered as 4000, was rebuilt as a 'Star' and it was to remain in this guise until rebuilt as a 'Castle' in November 1929. A Worcester-based locomotive for much of its career, it was transferred to Landore shortly before withdrawal in May 1957. *R. C. Riley Collection*

Left:
No **4016** *The Somerset Light Infantry (Prince Albert's)* is pictured at Chippenham at the head of a down train during its relatively brief career on BR. Rebuilt from 'Star' class No 4016 *Knight of the Golden Fleece* in October 1925, the locomotive was renamed on 18 February 1938 in a ceremony at Paddington station. Allocated to Newton Abbot for much of its later career, No 4016 was destined to be withdrawn from Old Oak Common in September 1951. *Kenneth Leech*

Right:
Another of the 'Star' rebuilds, No **4032** *Queen Alexandra*, was also one of the relatively early casualties, again being withdrawn in September 1951, this time from Taunton. Here the locomotive is seen at Chippenham with an up service. The locomotive, which had been converted from a 'Star' in April 1926, was to spend much of its career allocated to the West Country, normally being allocated to either Laira or Newton Abbot. *Kenneth Leech*

Above:

In June 1958, No **4037** *The South Wales Borderers* passes through Teignmouth with the up 'Devonian'. One of the first batch of 'Star' class 4-6-0s to be rebuilt as 'Castles', No 4037 emerged from Swindon Works in June 1926, one of only two members of the class that were constructed as rebuilds that year. Looking in fine condition — the cleaners at home shed Newton Abbot had certainly done their work — it would remain allocated to the Devon shed until a final transfer to Exeter in July 1962, from where it was withdrawn two months later. This locomotive is credited with the greatest mileage of any 'Castle', 2,479,722, including 776,764 as a 'Star'. The total mileages for almost all the rebuilds exceeded any 'Castle' proper, seven reaching 2 million miles. *L. Elsey*

Left:

By 1957, when this view of No **4073** *Caerphilly Castle* was taken at Bristol Bath Road shed, the prototype of the class was almost 35 years old. No 4073's home for the bulk of its career was Old Oak Common locomotive, moving to Bath Road in July 1950, staying there apart from three months at St Philips Marsh in 1952/3, until February 1957 when it was reallocated to Cardiff Canton. On withdrawal from Canton in May 1960 (having logged a recorded mileage of 1,910,730 — the fourth highest for any member of the class proper), the locomotive spent seven months at Swindon Works before being restored and preserved at the Science Museum (see pp110/1). The locomotive, still part of the National Collection, was removed from the Science Museum and can now be seen at Steam: Museum of the Great Western Railway at, appropriately, Swindon. *N. E. Preedy*

Right:
Pictured light engine at Royal Oak on 29 August 1959, shortly after being fitted with a double chimney (in April 1959), No 4074 *Caldicot Castle* was the second of the 'Castle' class to be constructed, emerging from Swindon Works in December 1923. Allocated when recorded here to Swansea (Landore), the locomotive would ultimately be based at Old Oak Common, from where it would be withdrawn in May 1963. *R. C. Riley*

Centre right:
On 16 May 1959 No 4075 *Cardiff Castle* is pictured at the head of the regular Glasgow/Manchester-Penzance service as it reaches the summit of the 1 in 71/80 climb out of Truro heading westwards. At this date the locomotive was allocated to Bristol Bath Road but would be transferred to Old Oak Common six months later. Never fitted with a double chimney, No 4075 was withdrawn from Old Oak Common in November 1961. *M. Mensing*

Below:
Taking the slow lines through Tilehurst on 1 August 1959, No 4076 *Carmarthen Castle* heads the 2.40pm service from Reading to Swindon. Allocated to Landore at the time, judging by the external condition of the locomotive, this was probably a running-in turn for a recently ex-Works locomotive. No 4076 remained at Landore until transferred to Llanelly in June 1961. The locomotive was withdrawn in February 1963. *R. C. Riley*

Left:
Pictured at Cowley Bridge Junction on 16 July 1958 No **4077** *Chepstow Castle* heads eastbound with the 12.20pm milk train from Penzance to Kensington. No 4077 was, at this time allocated to Laira, but was to be transferred to Newton Abbot in May 1959. Transferred again to Bristol Bath Road in February 1960, the locomotive's last reallocation took it to Bristol St Philips Marsh in September 1960, from where it would be withdrawn in August 1962. *R. C. Riley*

Below:
On 12 April 1958 'Castle' No **4078** *Pembroke Castle* double-heads a Bournemouth-Birkenhead service through Lapworth with 'Hall' No **4933** *Himley Hall*. At this date No 4078 was allocated to Chester, but it would move to Reading two months later. After passing through St Philips Marsh, Stafford Road, Banbury and Old Oak Common, No 4078's final shed, from June 1961 until withdrawal in July 1962, was Llanelly. *T. E. Williams/Courtesy National Railway Museum*

Right:

Pictured from the window of a down service at Bordesley on 23 April 1954, No **4079** *Pendennis Castle* makes a fine sight as it heads southwards with the up 5pm service from Snow Hill to Paddington. Undoubtedly one of the most famous members of the class, No 4079 had featured during the locomotive exchanges of 1925, having been constructed at Swindon Works in February 1924. By the date of this photograph, the locomotive was based at Stafford Road, where it would remain until transferred to Bristol Bath Road. Following spells at Taunton, Bristol St Philips Marsh and Swindon, No 4079 was withdrawn from St Philips Marsh in May 1964. Preserved on withdrawal, the locomotive has recently been repatriated to the UK after a spell in Australia and is now on display at the Didcot Railway Centre. *T. E. Williams/ Courtesy National Railway Museum*

Below:

No **4080** *Powderham Castle* is viewed on 18 March 1962 at the head of the 12.50 service from Cardiff to Brighton. The locomotive was built originally in March 1924 and had been fitted with a double chimney in August 1958. At the time that the locomotive was recorded, it was allocated to Cardiff Canton but was to be transferred to Cardiff East Dock in August 1962. It passed to Southall in September 1963 and, after brief sojourns to East Dock again and Old Oak Common, was to be withdrawn in August 1964. No 4080 was to achieve the highest recorded mileage of any 'Castle' proper (excluding rebuilt 'Stars'), reaching the grand total of 1,974,461 miles by the time that recording ceased on 28 December 1963. *Ivo Peters*

Left:

On 15 April 1953, No **4081** *Warwick Castle* climbs into Cockett Tunnel with a service from South Wales to Paddington. By this date No 4081 was already almost 30 years old, having been constructed originally in March 1924. Allocated to Landore, the locomotive would subsequently spend time at Exeter, Bristol Bath Road twice, Shrewsbury and Llanelly before a final transfer in July 1962 took it to Carmarthen. Withdrawal occurred in January the following year.
J. N. Westwood

Left:

In early 1952 King George VI died suddenly and the royal locomotive No **4082** *Windsor Castle* was again selected to have the honour of hauling the royal funeral train. Unfortunately, the original No 4082 was at Worcester shed awaiting repair. It was decided, therefore, that the identity of No 4082 would be swapped with 1948-built No 7013 *Bristol Castle*. On 15 February 1952 the 'new' No 4082 is pictured at Ealing Broadway with the royal funeral train. Once the swap had been effected, the locomotives never resumed their original identities as a result of a letter to *The Times* which had pointed BR's subterfuge (a sin compounded by the fact that a small cabside plate — subsequently removed — claimed that the locomotive had indeed been driven by the King, as Duke of York, on his visit to Swindon). As No 4082, the locomotive was allocated to Old Oak Common for much of its career, only being transferred to Gloucester Horton Road in August 1964, the month before it was withdrawn. *R. F. Roberts/ SLS Collection*

Left:

At 6.50pm on 28 May 1957, No **4083** *Abbotsbury Castle* heads northbound at Knowle & Dorridge station with the down 'Cornishman'. The stock for the train was in BR chocolate and cream livery, which had only recently been introduced to this service. At the date of the photograph, No 4083 was allocated to Stafford Road, followed by a period between April 1958 and September 1960 at Newton Abbot, and then spending a year at Exeter. A final transfer, in September 1961, saw the locomotive move to Cardiff Canton, from where it was withdrawn three months later. *M. Mensing*

Right:
A Bristol Bath Road locomotive for many years, No **4084** *Aberystwyth Castle* was captured outside Newton Abbot shed on 29 August 1954. No 4084 was transferred from Bath Road to Reading in November 1959, then on to Cardiff Canton two months later. No 4084 was to be withdrawn in October 1960 and cut up at Swindon the following month. Note above the locomotive, part of the weathervane formed of a locomotive which stood above Newton Abbot Works. *R. C. Riley*

Left:
On 20 June 1959 No **4085** *Berkeley Castle* departs from Gloucester with the 9.20am service to Paddington. At this time No 4085 was allocated to Gloucester, as evinced by its shed plate, although it had only been allocated there after a brief, month-long stay, in April-May 1958, at Worcester. After almost two years in Gloucester, it returned briefly to Worcester in March 1960 before a final transfer to Old Oak Common. No 4085 was withdrawn in May 1962. *T. E. Williams/Courtesy National Railway Museum*

Right:
Recorded near Patney, between Westbury and Pewsey, on 9 July 1956, Laira-allocated No **4086** *Builth Castle* heads eastbound with an up express, the relief to the 8.20am service from Penzance. No 4086 was to move to Swindon in April 1957 and to Reading in September 1959. After a period at Cardiff Canton, from December 1959 until May 1961, the locomotive returned to Reading, from where it was withdrawn in April 1962. No 4086 was to achieve fame as the first GWR locomotive to reach 100mph since the success of *City of Truro*. *R. C. Riley*

Left:
Allocated to Laira when recorded here outside its home shed on 4 June 1960, No **4087** *Cardigan Castle* had been fitted with a double chimney in February 1958. A further modification is also clearly evident: the presence of a mechanical lubrication equipment on the side of the smoke box.
No 4087 would remain at Laira until March 1963, when it was reallocated to Bristol St Philips Marsh, from where it was withdrawn during the following October. *P. H. Groom*

Right:
Viewed at Paddington in March 1959, No **4088** *Dartmouth Castle* had been fitted with a double chimney in May 1958. A Worcester-based locomotive when recorded, it was to be transferred to Swindon in February 1961 and to Bristol St Philips Marsh in October 1963. Withdrawal came in May 1964. *N. E. Preedy*

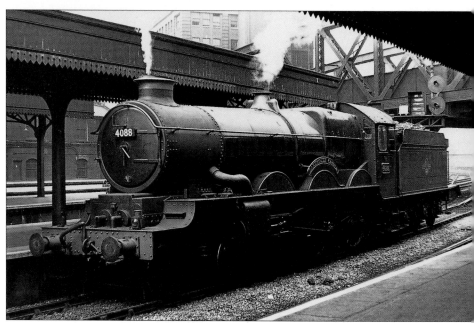

Left:
The arrival of the 'Britannia' class Pacifics was to result in 4-6-2s appearing regularly at Paddington but many of the most prestigious services continued to the powered by ex-GWR 4-6-0s. On 4 August 1952 the new order is demonstrated by 'Britannia' No 70018 *Flying Dutchman* although it is 'Castle' No **4089** *Donnington Castle* that is at the head of 'The Red Dragon' for Cardiff and Swansea. Allocated at this time to Plymouth Laira, No 4089 would ultimately end its days allocated to Reading from where it was withdrawn in October 1964, one of the last non-double chimney locomotives to remain in service. *R. C. Riley*

Above:
After experiments with No 7018, No **4090** *Dorchester Castle* was the first of the class, in April 1957, to be fitted with a double chimney. It is pictured here, on 20 April 1957, on Hatton Bank with the down 'Cambrian Coast Express'. At this time the locomotive was allocated to Old Oak Common, but it would be transferred via Landore, Carmarthen, Landore (again), Neath and Shrewsbury before ending its career at Cardiff East Dock, to which it was allocated in September 1962. No 4090 was finally withdrawn in June 1963. *R. C. Riley*

Right:
Recorded at Paddington on 30 August 1958, No **4091** *Dudley Castle* has one particular claim to fame in the 'Castle' story: apart from the rebuilt locomotives, it was the first of the class to be withdrawn, succumbing only five months after this photograph was taken, in January 1959 (possibly as a result of the accident damage received in World War 2). As is evident from the shedplate, the locomotive was allocated to Old Oak Common.
R. C. Riley

Left:
Recorded at speed near Solihull on
21 June 1961, No **4092** *Dunraven
Castle* was providing the motive power
for the 6.45am service from
Wolverhampton (Low Level) to
Paddington. By this date, No 4092
was in the twilight of its career;
allocated to Oxford, the locomotive
was destined to be withdrawn during
December 1961. *M. Mensing*

Above:
By 9 February 1964, when this view of No **4093** *Dunster
Castle* in the company of No 7813 was taken at Reading
shed, time was rapidly running out for the remaining
members of the 'Castle' class. Indeed No 4093 itself would
succumb later the same year, when it was withdrawn in

September from Gloucester Horton Road. When recorded
here, however, the locomotive was allocated to Bristol St
Philips Marsh, to where it had been transferred from
Llanelly in March 1963. No 4093 had been one of the
earliest of the class to be fitted with a double chimney,
being so fitted in December 1957. *J. R. Carter*

Left:
Pictured at Newton Abbot on 29 August 1954, No **4094** *Dynevor Castle* heads westbound with the down 'Cornishman'. Never fitted with a double chimney, No 4094 was to be withdrawn from Carmarthen Shed in March 1962. In the 50 years since this photograph was taken, Newton Abbot has undergone considerable rationalisation, with the northernmost platforms taken out of use and the signalboxes replaced; much of this rationalisation took place in the late 1980s when the semaphore signalling was replaced. On the extreme right, the site is now part of the publishing offices of the well-known firm of David & Charles. *R. C. Riley*

Centre right:
Although, by 27 August 1950, when the locomotive was recorded at Landore shed, No **4095** *Harlech Castle* had acquired a smokebox number plate, it still had no BR identification on the tender. At this time Landore represented the locomotive's home shed, but it would see life at Penzance (from December 1957), Taunton (from May 1960) and Laira (from June 1960) before withdrawal from Reading, to which it had been allocated in September 1962, in December 1962. Never fitted with a double chimney, the locomotive was destined to end its career well away from its traditional home, being one of only five of the class to be scrapped by King's of Norwich. *A. A. G. Delicato*

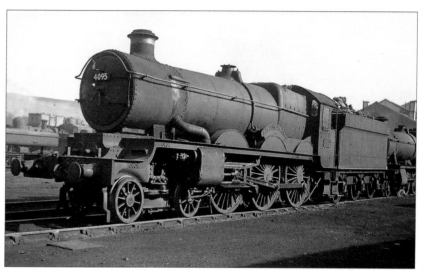

Lower right:
No **4096** *Highclere Castle* was ultimately to achieve the second-highest recorded mileage — 1,958,378 miles — of a 'Castle' proper before its withdrawal in January 1963. A decade earlier, on 22 August 1952, the locomotive was helping to clock up the miles when it was recorded at the head of the 2.33pm service from Portsmouth to Bristol near Wilton North. No 4096 was a Bristol Bath Road locomotive for many years, before being transferred to Old Oak Common in March 1958. In July 1962 it was reallocated to Reading and then back again to Old Oak Common in the following December. The following month it was transferred, briefly, to Llanelly, from where it was withdrawn. *R. F. Roberts/SLS Collection*

45

Above:
On 26 September 1953, No **4097** *Kenilworth Castle* heads westwards with a down service from Paddington at Southall. An Old Oak Common locomotive at this date, No 4097 would be transferred to Landore in 1957. One of the earliest casualties amongst the production 'Castles' No 4097 would be withdrawn from Landore in May 1960. *B. Y. Williams*

Left:
Displaying its 83A shedplate, No **4098** *Kidwelly Castle* is recorded at its home shed on 19 July 1958. Constructed in July 1926 and never fitted with a double chimney, No 4098 remained at Newton Abbot until July 1962 when it was transferred to Old Oak Common, from where it was withdrawn in December 1963. *R. C. Riley*

Right:
Recorded at Bristol Bath Road shed, in May 1952, No **4099** *Kilgerran Castle* was, at the time, allocated to Newton Abbot. After a brief spell at Penzance, No 4099 was transferred to Landore in October 1957 and then to Neath in June 1961 and finally to Llanelly in July 1962, from where it was withdrawn two months later.
J. Davenport

Centre right:
Pictured at Ruabon on 5 July 1952 with an up special, No **5000** *Launceston Castle* had been built originally in September 1926. Allocated to Bristol Bath Road when recorded here, the locomotive would spend many years based at Swindon before being transferred in May 1962 to Gloucester and thence to Hereford in October 1963. It was transferred to the LMR, based at Oxley, in June 1964, from where it was withdrawn in October of the same year. For those who know Ruabon, this photograph will bring back memories of the facilities once provided at this important junction and give a sad reflection on the rudimentary provision in the 21st century.
R. W. Hinton

Lower right:
Recorded heading towards Chester at Saltney Junction on 9 May 1959 at the head of the 6am service from Birmingham Snow Hill to Birkenhead, No **5001** *Llandovery Castle* makes a fine sight as it approaches the photographer. By this date No 5001 was allocated to Shrewsbury; a final transfer, in August 1960, would see it move to Old Oak Common, from where it was withdrawn in February 1963. No 5001 was fitted with a double chimney in July 1961.
S. D. Wainwright

Above:

With the Cirencester branch platform immediately behind it, No **5002** *Ludlow Castle* passes through Kemble station with the 6.55am service from Cheltenham on 9 June 1962. Allocated at this time to Swindon, No 5002 would be transferred to Bristol St Philips Marsh in November 1963, to Reading in April 1964 and, finally, to Southall two months later. No 5002 was withdrawn in September 1964. *Ivo Peters*

Left:

In 1955 No **5003** *Lulworth Castle* was recorded at the head of the relief to the 6.55am Wolverhampton to Paignton service. Allocated to Exeter, No 5003 would subsequently pass via Laira, Exeter again, Laira again, Carmarthen and Cardiff Canton before its final reallocation to Newton Abbot in March 1959, from where it was withdrawn in August 1962. Note that, whilst the locomotive has been provided with a headboard, it has been reversed so that the blank side is displayed. The story told locally at Newton Abbot on the locomotive's withdrawal was that, when prepared for its final departure, the locomotive had no fire irons; a quick search of the yard found some and so No 5003 was able to depart, bringing to an end the steam era at Newton Abbot.

Ian Allan Library

Above:

In low winter sunlight, No **5004** *Llanstephan Castle* heads towards Paddington with an up service at West Drayton on 9 December 1949. Note that, although the locomotive has received its BR numberplate, it is still without a shed plate. At the time, No 5004 was an Old Oak Common locomotive but would later see service at Shrewsbury, from June 1956, and then be reallocated via Cardiff Canton and Landore, before its final shed — Neath — from where it was withdrawn in April 1962.

T. E. Williams/Courtesy National Railway Museum

Right:

At the head of a down express service to South Wales on 20 August 1955, No **5005** *Manorbier Castle* passes Old Oak Common East. As is evident from the shed plate on the locomotive, No 5005 was allocated to Cardiff Canton (86C). Transferred to Newton Abbot, then Old Oak Common and Swindon, No 5005 made a brief return to Canton in June 1959 before a final transfer back to Swindon the following month, from where it was withdrawn in February 1960. No 5005 was never fitted with a double chimney. *R. C. Riley*

Left:
It's June 1954 and the wild flowers on the embankment are in full bloom as No **5006** *Tregenna Castle* swings into the station loop at Badminton with the down 'Red Dragon' bound for Cardiff and Swansea. Allocated to Cardiff Canton at the time, No 5006 would be transferred to Old Oak Common before returning to Wales — Carmarthen — in April 1958. Allocated to Landore between July 1960 and June 1961, No 5006 was then briefly allocated to Llanelly before returning to Carmarthen in September 1961, from where it was withdrawn in April 1962.
George F. Heiron

Centre left:
A well-polished No **5007** *Rougemont Castle* awaits its duty on the up 'Red Dragon' at Cardiff General on 13 May 1952. Although the service only started at Swansea, the locomotive was replaced at Cardiff. The reason for this relatively short working for the Swansea crew was that, if they had worked through to Paddington, it would have been a lodging turn, whilst for Cardiff-based crews it was possible to get to and from Paddington in a single roster. At this time, No 5007 was based at Cardiff Canton and so will have been well-cleaned by the loco cleaners at its home shed before coming into service. No 5007, never fitted with a double chimney, was transferred to Old Oak Common in March 1957 and to Swindon in February 1959. A further transfer, in March 1961, saw it move to Gloucester, from where it was withdrawn in September 1962.
R. C. Riley

Lower left:
On 2 September 1962, No **5008** *Raglan Castle* can be seen picking up water as it passes over Ruislip troughs at the head of the 6.10pm service from Paddington to Shrewsbury. No 5008 had been fitted with a double chimney in March the previous year and, by this date, was allocated to Old Oak Common. This must have been one of the last workings for No 5008 as the locomotive was to be withdrawn shortly afterwards. *M. Pope*

Above:

In 1952, BR constructed two Hawksworth-pattern tenders fitted with coal self-weighing apparatus: No 4127 in lined green and No 4128 in lined black. These tenders had a capacity of 3,800gal of water plus six tons of coal and weighed a total of 49tons 18cwt when full. The tenders were used on a range of ex-GWR types, including the 'Castles'. Here No **5009** *Shrewsbury Castle* is seen with the green-liveried tender. A Swindon-allocated locomotive throughout the 1950s, No 5009 would be withdrawn from there in October 1960. *J. D. Mills/R. C. Riley Collection*

Right:

Recorded in June 1953, No **5010** *Restormel Castle* is seen near High Wycombe with the down 11.10am service from Paddington to Birkenhead. Allocated by this date to Stafford Road, No 5010 was to be transferred to Old Oak Common in March 1958, then on to Reading in January 1959, from where it was to be withdrawn that October, one of only three of the class to succumb that year. When allocated to Cardiff Canton, No 5010 was noted as a 'rogue' locomotive and crews were particularly reluctant to take it on the North & West route. Perhaps when they got an allocation of 'Britannia' Class Pacifics they took the chance to transfer it away. Its reputation was possibly borne out by its relatively early demise. *Brian Morrison*

Left:
Newton Abbot-allocated No **5011** *Tintagel Castle* is pictured at its home station with a westbound service. No 5011 was to remain allocated to 83A until May 1960 when it was transferred to Reading. In October 1960 a further transfer saw the locomotive move to Old Oak Common. Never fitted with a double chimney, No 5011 was exactly 35 years old when withdrawn from 81A in September 1962. *R. Hewitt*

Right:
On 9 May 1959, No **5012** *Berry Pomeroy Castle* heads westbound at Saltney Junction with a service from Birkenhead to Bournemouth. Allocated to Oxford, No 5012 would survive in service until April 1962. *S. D. Wainwright*

Below:
With driver Jack Hayward, alongside fireman Denis Guyatt, at the controls, No **5013** *Abergavenny Castle* stands at Bath on 4 November 1955. Built in June 1932, No 5013 was by this time allocated to Landore, where it would remain until transferred to Neath in December 1961. Its career at Neath was to be relatively short, being withdrawn from there the following July. *Kenneth Leech*

Right:
Pictured at Dorridge on 26 August 1951, No **5014** *Goodrich Castle* was built originally in June 1932. Allocated to Old Oak Common for much of its career, No 5014 was transferred to Tyseley in June 1964 for the last months of its career, being withdrawn in February 1965.
C. F. H. Oldham

Below:
By 21 February 1963, when it was recorded entering Hereford with the 9.30am service from Manchester, No **5015** *Kingswear Castle* was approaching the end of its 30-year career. Built in July 1932, in September 1962 the locomotive was transferred to Cardiff East Dock from where it was withdrawn in April 1963.
A. A. Vickers

Left:
With the locomotive crew's attention firmly caught by something on the embankment, No **5016** *Montgomery Castle* enters Cockett Tunnel with an eastbound slow passenger service. No 5016, allocated to Landore for much of its career, was originally built in July 1932 and was to be fitted with a double chimney in early 1961. It was transferred to Llanelly in June 1961, from where it was withdrawn in September the following year.
J. N. Westwood

Below left:
In April 1954, No **5017**, originally named *St Donat's Castle*, was renamed *The Gloucestershire Regiment 28th/61st*. The locomotive is seen here, on 13 May 1954, shortly after the renaming, with the new plates prominently displayed. Note also the regimental symbol attached to the splasher. No 5017 was, appropriately, allocated to Gloucester shed for its latter years, being withdrawn from there in September 1962.
Ian Allan Library

Above right:
On 1 August 1953 No **5018** *St Mawes Castle* heads the 11.30am up service from Cheltenham through Sonning. This locomotive, originally built in July 1932, was a Gloucester-allocated locomotive at this stage. It would be transferred to Reading in April 1958, remaining in service at that shed until March 1964. *A. R. Carpenter*

Right:
No **5019** *Treago Castle* storms under the familiar Bishop's Bridge Road bridge as it departs from Paddington with the 1.15pm service to Bristol. A Bristol Bath Road-allocated locomotive for much of its career, No 5019 would end its career at Wolverhampton Stafford Road, in September 1962, having been reallocated there in April 1958. No 5019 was to receive a double chimney in February 1961. *R. C. Riley*

Left:
Pictured at its home shed of Cardiff Canton (a shed which vied with Worcester for the cleanliness of its locomotives), on 26 July 1952, No **5020** *Trematon Castle* was exactly 20 years old when recorded here, having been completed at Swindon in July 1932. No 5020 remained at Cardiff until November 1957 when it was transferred to Laira and thence to Penzance in December the following year. Following a further three moves between May 1960 and September 1961, No 5020 was reallocated, for the last time, to Llanelly, in August 1962, from where it was withdrawn three months later. *R. C. Riley*

Centre left:
No **5021** *Whittington Castle* is pictured at Par on 14 July 1955 with the down 'Cornishman'. Allocated to Exeter at this time, No 5021 would be transferred to Laira in March 1957 and to Cardiff in September 1959. Apart from a month at Bristol St Philips Marsh in late 1960, No 5021 would see out the remainder of its career at Cardiff, being withdrawn in September 1962. *Ray Hinton*

Right:
Seen on Ruislip troughs on 2 August 1958, No **5022** *Wigmore Castle* was providing the motive power for the relief portion of the 6.10pm service from Paddington to Birkenhead. Apart from a month at Old Oak Common early in 1956, No 5022 was allocated throughout the 1950s and early 1960s, to Wolverhampton Stafford Road, until its withdrawal in June 1963. No 5022 was fitted with a double chimney in March 1959. *C. R. L. Coles/Rail Archive Stephenson*

Above:
On 21 October 1951 N0 **5023** *Brecon Castle* is pictured having just passed Thingley Junction with the 'Cornish Riviera' express. The train had been diverted via Bristol as a result of emergency engineering work on the Westbury route. No 5023 was ultimately to be allocated to Swindon, from where it was withdrawn in February 1963.
G. J. Jefferson

Right:
With the station nameboard providing a poignant reminder as to how much of the railway network has disappeared over the past 45 years, Taunton station provides the backdrop for this view of No **5024** *Carew Castle* on 12 May 1958 as it heads towards Bristol with the 8am service from Plymouth to Crewe. Allocated at the time to Newton Abbot, No 5024 would be withdrawn from that shed in May 1962.
Brian Morrison

Left:
On 19 May 1957 No **5025** *Chirk Castle* heads eastwards at Rumney Bridge (Cardiff) with the 4.10pm milk train from Whitland to Kensington. This duty was a Swindon diagram and No 5025 was recorded whilst running in after repair at the works. No 5025 was, at this time, allocated to Swindon, but would be transferred to Oxford in April the following year. In October 1963 it was reallocated to Hereford, from where it was withdrawn the following month. *R. O. Tuck*

Right:
On 5 November 1962, Wolverhampton Stafford Road-allocated No **5026** *Criccieth Castle* stands at Chester. Fitted with a double chimney in October 1959, No 5026 was transferred to the second Wolverhampton shed, Oxley, in September 1963, from where it was withdrawn in November of the following year. *J. R. Carter*

Left:
The 7.50am service for Fishguard Harbour departs from Newport High Street on 11 July 1952 behind No **5027** *Farleigh Castle*. A Wolverhampton Stafford Road locomotive at this date, No 5027 would be subsequently allocated to Bristol Bath Road before transfer to Old Oak Common in April 1958. Following the fitting of a double chimney in March 1961, the locomotive was to be transferred in July 1961 to Carmarthen. A final transfer, in July 1962, saw No 5027 move to Llanelly, from where it was withdrawn in November the same year. *R. C. Riley*

Right:
Pictured at Wellington, in Somerset, at the head of a service from Manchester to Plymouth, No **5028** *Llantilio Castle* was at this stage allocated to Newton Abbot. Transferred to Laira in June 1956, it was withdrawn in May 1960 never having been fitted with a double chimney. *Ian Allan Library*

Above:
No doubt the locomotive has been specially cleaned for the occasion as, amongst the passengers on board the 2.15pm service from Paddington to Gloucester on 12 October 1957, was HRH Princess Margaret. The train, headed by No **5029** *Nunney Castle,* is seen passing Old Oak Common East signalbox. Allocated to 81A, No 5029 moved to Worcester in April 1958 and then had spells at Shrewsbury, Newton Abbot and Laira before a final transfer, in December 1962 took it to Cardiff East Dock, from where it was withdrawn in December 1963. After a period of storage, No 5029 was sold to Woodham Bros at Barry in June 1964, where it was to languish for 12 years before rescue by the Great Western Society in 1976. Restoration to main line condition followed at the GWS's museum at Didcot. *R. C. Riley*

Above:

On 21 June 1951 No **5030** *Shirburn Castle* passes Onibury with an express from Plymouth to Manchester. Apart from the smokebox numberplate and 86C shedplate, three years after Nationalisation, the scene is still almost pure Great Western. Note also the clerestory coach forming the lead vehicle in the consist. No 5030 was allocated to Cardiff Canton. It would be transferred to Carmarthen in August 1958 and, apart from a brief spell at Landore in 1960, would spend the rest of its career allocated there. No 5030 was withdrawn in September 1962. *C. R. L. Coles/Rail Archive Stephenson*

Left:

Heading southbound through High Wycombe on 23 September 1954, No **5031** *Totnes Castle* heads the up 'Inter City' from Birmingham to Paddington. Allocated to Wolverhampton Stafford Road for much of its career, No 5031, which was fitted with a double chimney in May 1959, was transferred to Oxley in September 1963, from where it was withdrawn the following month. *Ian Allan Library*

Above:

Towards the end of its journey, No **5032** *Usk Castle* passes Old Oak Common with the up 2pm service from Wolverhampton on 3 September 1955. No 5032 was, by this date allocated to Stafford Road, having originally been based at Shrewsbury from new. In April 1958 it was transferred to Newton Abbot and in March 1960 to Old Oak Common, from where it was withdrawn in September 1962. A double chimney was fitted in May 1959. *R. C. Riley*

Right:

Recorded in ex-Works condition at Swindon on 16 October 1960, No **5033** *Broughton Castle* had only just been outshopped following the fitting of its double chimney. Having been transferred to Oxford in June 1958, No 5033 was to be withdrawn from there in September 1962.
Ian Allan Library

Left:
Despite appearances to the contrary, this is not the 'Torbay Express', although the headboard's presence on the smokebox of No **5034** _Corfe Castle_ on 18 July 1958 would seem to indicate otherwise. The locomotive is seen at Aller Junction with a freight having worked the down express earlier in the day. Aller Junction box would survive for a further 30 years, not being demolished until the late 1980s. No 5034 was, when recorded here, allocated to Old Oak Common, and would remain there until final withdrawal in September 1962. The locomotive was one of the last to be fitted with a double chimney, being so treated in February 1961. _R. C. Riley_

Above:
A couple of youthful enthusiasts peer onto the footplate of No **5035** _Coity Castle_ at Birmingham (Snow Hill) on 3 January 1957 as the locomotive prepares to depart from the station with the down 'Cambrian Coast Express'.

No 5035 was allocated at this time to Old Oak Common and would be transferred to Swindon in September 1960, shortly before it was fitted with a double chimney (in December of that year). No 5035 would survive in service until May 1962. _M. Mensing_

Right:

On 6 November 1956, No **5036** *Lyonshall Castle* begins the descent of Hatton Bank with the through Birkenhead-Margate/Hastings service. Allocated to Old Oak Common for much of its career, by 1956 No 5036 had been transferred to Reading. It was to remain at Reading until a final transfer in October 1960 saw it migrate back to Old Oak Common. No 5036 was to be fitted with a double chimney two months later and was to be withdrawn in September 1962. *M. Mensing*

Right:

The 1.45pm service from Paddington to Worcester passes Old Oak Common on 3 September 1955 with No **5037** *Monmouth Castle* providing the motive power. As is evident from the shed plate, 85A (Worcester), the locomotive was returning to its home patch. It would remain at Worcester until transfer to Old Oak Common in June 1961 and thence to Neath the following month. After brief spells at Llanelly (twice) and Neath again, the locomotive's final shed was Bristol St Philips Marsh, to which it was allocated in October 1963. Never fitted with a double chimney, No 5037 was to be withdrawn in March 1964. *R. C. Riley*

Left:

Pictured at Bristol in 1948, shortly after Nationalisation, this photograph of No **5037** *Monmouth Castle* is of note in that it shows the locomotive in full GWR livery but with 'British Railways' on the tender in GWR-style lettering. *Ian Allan Library*

Above:
Approaching Thingley Junction on 7 February 1951, No **5038** *Morlais Castle* is providing the motive power for the up 12 noon express from Bristol to Paddington. An Old Oak Common locomotive for much of its career, No 5038 was transferred to Shrewsbury in April 1958. In May 1962 No 5038 was reallocated to Oxford and, five months later a further move saw it transferred to Reading. The locomotive was withdrawn from Reading the following September. *G. J. Jefferson*

Below:
In January 1964 No **5039** *Rhuddlan Castle* was transferred to Reading shed, its fifth shed in less than 18 months. Shortly before this final transfer, one of its last duties when allocated to Cardiff Canton was on 25 January 1964 when it hauled a football excursion northwards from Cardiff. The train is pictured passing Church Stretton. The locomotive would be based at Reading for barely six months, being withdrawn in June 1964. *Paul Riley*

Above:
No **5040** *Stokesay Castle* speeds past Bentley Heath Crossing, near Knowle & Dorridge station, with an up return excursion from Wolverhampton to Paddington on 5 July 1959. This locomotive was allocated to Old Oak Common for much of its career, but was to be transferred to Bristol Bath Road in October 1961. It was withdrawn from Bath Road exactly two years later. *M. Mensing*

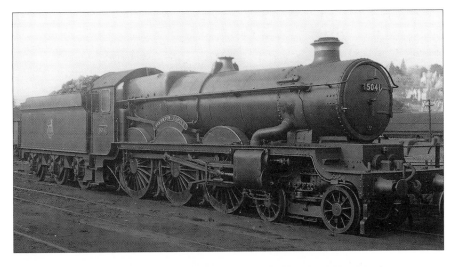

Centre right:
Newton Abbot-allocated No **5041** *Tiverton Castle* is pictured on shed awaiting its next duty in the early 1950s. The locomotive was subsequently to be allocated to Llanelly and, after a brief spell at Neath between June 1961 and July the following, was to end its days at Old Oak Common, succumbing in December 1963. *F. W. Day*

Lower right:
On 6 August 1960, HRH Prince Charles and HRH Princess Anne travelled in the rear saloon of the down 'Cambrian Coast Express'. The presence of royalty on board helps to explain both the immaculate condition of No **5042** *Winchester Castle* and also interest in the train evinced by members of the Ranelagh Bridge enginemen visible on the right. No 5042 had been transferred to Old Oak Common in April 1960 and was to remain there until transferred to Newton Abbot in July 1962. It was withdrawn from Gloucester in June 1965, having never been fitted with a double chimney.
R. C. Riley

Above:
Recorded in 1951, No **5043** *Earl of Mount Edgcumbe* looks in fine external condition. Built originally in March 1936, No 5043 carried the name *Barbury Castle* until September 1937. The locomotive was fitted with a double chimney in May 1958, when allocated to Old Oak Common. In April 1962 the locomotive was transferred to Cardiff Canton and then to Cardiff East Dock the following August. No 5043 was withdrawn from East Dock in December 1963 and was then sold to Woodham Bros scrapyard. After almost a decade at Barry, No 5043 was rescued in August 1973 by the Birmingham Railway Museum, originally as a source of spares. It remains on display at Tyseley. *Ian Allan Library*

Below:
The driver of No **5044** *Earl of Dunraven* looks back as he cautiously reverses the locomotive into Old Oak Common on 20 May 1956. This remained No 5044's home shed until August 1960 when it migrated to Cardiff Canton, where it stayed — except for two months in 1961 when it was allocated to Neath — until withdrawal in April 1962. Originally named *Beverston Castle*, the locomotive was renamed in September 1937. *R. C. Riley*

Above:
In September 1954 No **5045** *Earl of Dudley* heads southbound near Harefield with an up service from Birmingham to Paddington. Allocated to Wolverhampton Stafford Road at the time, No 5045 would remain based there until withdrawal in September 1962. The locomotive was one of the class not to be fitted with a double chimney. No 5045 had originally been named *Bridgwater Castle*, but was renamed *Earl of Dudley* in September 1937. *Ian Allan Library*

Below:
Heading southwards over the North & West route approaching Marshbrook, between Shrewsbury and Hereford, in 1951, No **5046** *Earl Cawdor* was at the head of the 3pm service from Liverpool. Named *Clifford Castle* until August 1937, No 5046 was a Cardiff Canton locomotive for much of its career, being transferred to Wolverhampton Stafford Road in April 1958, from where it was withdrawn in September 1962. *C. R. L. Coles/Rail Archive Stephenson*

Left:
Judging by the smoke, the fireman has been busy on the footplate of No **5047** *Earl of Dartmouth* as it heads north with the main (ex-Penzance portion) of the 'Cornishman' at 6.52pm on 15 June 1957. The train is nearing the summit of Wilmcote Bank to the north of Stratford-on-Avon. No 5047 was named *Compton Castle* until August 1937. The locomotive was allocated by 1957 to Stafford Road, from where it was withdrawn in August 1962. *M. Mensing*

Above:
On 9 August 1955, No **5048** *Earl of Devon* stands at Chippenham with an up service to Paddington. Built in April 1936, No 5048 was named *Cranbrook Castle* until August 1937. A Bristol Bath Road-based locomotive virtually throughout its career, No 5048 was to remain there until transferred to St Philips Marsh in September 1960.

Two months later a further move saw No 5048 transferred to Cardiff Canton and, the following October, a further move saw it allocated to Neath. In August 1962, No 5048 was transferred for a final time — to Llanelly — but this was to be short-lived as the locomotive was withdrawn the same month. *Kenneth Leech*

Above:
Recorded at Stoneycombe on 3 July 1957, No **5049** *Earl of Plymouth* — named *Denbigh Castle* until August 1937 — heads eastwards with the up 'Royal Duchy'. Allocated at this date to Laira, No 5049 would move to Newton Abbot in June 1958 and, following the fitting of a double chimney in August 1959, to Bristol Bath Road in May 1960. The locomotive was transferred to St Philips Marsh in September 1960, from where it was withdrawn in March 1963. *R. C. Riley*

Left:
No **5050** *Earl of St Germans* is seen at Swindon in February 1958 in ex-Works condition. Originally named *Devizes Castle*, No 5050 was renamed in August 1937. Allocated to Shrewsbury at this date, No 5050 was transferred to Old Oak Common in September 1960 and then to Bristol St Philips Marsh exactly a year later. The locomotive was withdrawn in August 1963. *G. Wheeler*

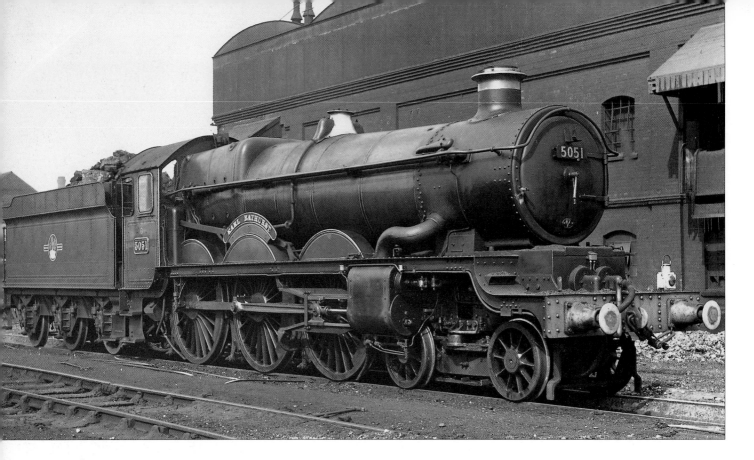

Above:

Fully coaled up, No **5051** *Earl Bathurst* awaits its next duty at Old Oak Common on 21 September 1958. Originally named *Drysllwyn Castle*, the locomotive's change of identity came in August 1937. A Landore-allocated engine when recorded, No 5051 was transferred to Neath in June 1961 and to Llanelly in February 1963, from where it was withdrawn in May 1963. After a period of storage at Llanelly, the locomotive was sold for scrap in February 1964 and passed to Woodham Bros at Barry. Rescued from the scrapyard by the Great Western Society, No 5051 was transferred to Didcot in February 1970 and has subsequently been fully restored. *R. C. Riley*

Above:

Awaiting its next turn at Old Oak Common on 29 August 1959 is No **5052** *Earl of Radnor*. The locomotive had been transferred to 81A from Cardiff Canton in January 1957 and was destined to remain there until a move to Bristol St Philips Marsh in September 1960. Never fitted with a double chimney, No 5052 was withdrawn in September 1962. No 5052 had originally been named *Eastnor Castle* until July 1937. *R. C. Riley*

Above:
A superb period shot, full of atmosphere, records the scene at the eastern end of Exeter St Davids on 20 July 1956 as the down 'Devonian' arrives in the station double-headed by No **5053** *Earl Cairns* and 'Hall' class No 6917 *Oldlands Hall*. In the foreground can be seen ex-LBSCR Class E1/R No 32135 standing in the Southern Region banking siding.

No 5053 had originally been named *Bishop's Castle*, but was renamed *Earl Cairns* in August 1937. No 5053 was, for many years, allocated to Wolverhampton Stafford Road, before transfer to Newton Abbot. From there it moved to Laira in November 1959 and Cardiff Canton in September 1961, from where it was withdrawn during the following July. *R. C. Riley*

Right:
Recorded as it moves off Bristol Bath Road shed, No **5054** *Earl of Ducie* was heading to Temple Meads station to provide the motive power for the up 'Great Western' to London Paddington. Alongside the 'Castle' is evidence of the Western Region's new order, in the guise of two 'Warships', including No D848 *Sultan*, and a single NBL B-B. The locomotive, named *Lamphey Castle* until September 1937, was allocated at this time to Worcester, from February until September 1964, when it was transferred to Gloucester; it was withdrawn in the next month.
N. E. Preedy

Above:
Originally named *Lydford Castle*, No **5055** was renamed *Earl of Eldon* in August 1937. The locomotive is pictured here passing through Teignmouth station on 17 July 1958 with the up 'Devonian' service. the locomotive had only recently been reallocated to Newton Abbot, in April 1958.

It remained allocated there until transferred to Carmarthen in January 1963. That year was eventful for the locomotive seeing two further transfers — to Goodwick and Hereford — before a final move saw it reallocated to Gloucester in July 1964. No 5055 was withdrawn in October 1964.
R. C. Riley

Left:
On 2 September 1962 immaculate No **5056** *Earl of Powis* stands at its home shed, Old Oak Common, fully coaled and ready for its next train. Waiting in the wings, however are the usurpers, in the shape of 'Warship' and 'Western' hydraulics which would eventually see off steam on the Western Region. New in June 1936, No 5056 had originally been named *Ogmore Castle*, but had been renamed in September 1937. A long-term resident of Old Oak Common, No 5056 would be transferred to Cardiff East Dock in July 1963, to Hereford in February 1964 and finally to Wolverhampton Stafford Road in June, from where it would be withdrawn five months later.
R. C. Riley

Left:
Originally named, until October 1937, *Penrice Castle*, No **5057** *Earl Waldegrave* was in immaculate condition when pictured at Gloucester Central on 11 April 1956. A Bristol Bath Road locomotive, No 5057 moved to Banbury in November 1959, having been fitted with a double chimney in May 1958, and then, in April 1960, to Old Oak Common from where it was withdrawn in March 1964, *P. J. Sharpe*

Right:
Laira-allocated No **5058** *Earl of Clancarty* is seen at Plymouth station in May 1961. Allocated to the West Country — either Newton Abbot or Laira — for most of its career, No 5058 — named *Newport Castle* until September 1937 — would be reallocated in September 1961 to Gloucester Horton Road for the last years of its career, being withdrawn in March 1963. *A. MacPherson*

Left:
Pictured at Teignmouth, No **5059** *Earl St Aldwyn* heads the up 'Devonian' on 2 July 1957. No 5059 was originally named *Powis Castle*, being given its new name in October 1937. The locomotive was, at this time, allocated to Newton Abbot, but would be transferred to Wolverhampton Stafford Road during the following year and then on to Shrewsbury in June 1959 from where it was withdrawn in June 1962. *R. C. Riley*

Above:

In 1956 the Russian Bolshoi Ballet company visited the British Isles and, on 4 November, a double-headed special, powered by Nos **5060** *Earl of Berkeley* and 5065 *Newport Castle*, provided transport to the troupe for their journey to Stratford. The train, with a suitable headboard, is seen approaching its destination. No 5060 was originally named *Sarum Castle* when constructed in June 1937, but was to be renamed four months later. Allocated to Old Oak Common, No 5060 was fitted with a double chimney in August 1958 and was to be withdrawn from 81A in April 1963. *T. E. Williams/Courtesy National Railway Museum*

Below:

Heading northwards at Hinksey South, between Radley and Oxford, No **5061** *Earl of Birkenhead* provides the motive power for a service from Margate to Birkenhead on 15 August 1959. Named originally, until October 1937, *Sudeley Castle*, No 5061 was a Reading-allocated locomotive when recorded here. It was transferred to Cardiff Canton in December 1959 from where it was withdrawn in September 1962. The photograph records the locomotive in double-chimney form, the modification having been carried out in August 1958. *R. C. Riley*

Above:

Heading westbound into Exeter St Davids on 23 June 1950 No **5062** *Earl of Shaftesbury* had been named *Tenby Castle* until November 1937. Allocated to Newton Abbot when new, the locomotive moved to Exeter in May 1950, Taunton in February 1951 and Swindon in October 1952, before passing to Bristol Bath Road in March 1958, to Llanelly in September 1960, Neath in June 1961 and Llanelly again in August 1962. It was withdrawn from Llanelly the next month. *C. F. H. Oldham*

Below:

On 10 July 1958, No **5063** *Earl Baldwin* is recorded as it approaches Knowle & Dorridge station with the 4.10pm service from Paddington to Wolverhampton. Named *Thornbury Castle* until July 1937, No 5063 was transferred to Stafford Road in May 1958. It was to remain based there until 84A closed in September 1963, when it migrated to Oxley for the remainder of its career. The locomotive was withdrawn in February 1965. *M. Mensing*

Left:
Looking in superb condition, No **5064** *Bishop's Castle* powers towards London with the 8.20am from Weston-super-Mare on 2 April 1955. Originally named *Tretower Castle*, the locomotive gained its new identity in September 1937. Allocated in 1955 to Bristol Bath Road, No 5064 would be transferred to Swindon in March 1958 and finally to Gloucester Horton Road in September 1961 having been fitted with a double chimney in September 1958. The locomotive was withdrawn in September 1962. *T. E. Williams/Courtesy National Railway Museum*

Below left:
On a bright summer's day, 5 July 1959, No **5065** *Newport Castle* rushes through Lapworth station with the up 'Inter-City' express for Paddington. Built in July 1937, No 5065 was originally named *Upton Castle*, but it bore this name for only two months before inheriting its later name from No 5058. An Old Oak Common locomotive throughout its post-Nationalisation career, No 5065 was eventually to be withdrawn in January 1963. *T. E. Williams/ Courtesy National Railway Museum*

Above:
Recorded at Old Oak Common on 16 August 1959, No **5066** *Sir Felix Pole* had been fitted with a double chimney only four months earlier. Until 24 April 1956, the locomotive had been named *Wardour Castle*, but was renamed after the General Manager of the GWR between June 1921 and July 1929 in a ceremony held at Paddington station. The new nameplates were unveiled by the late Sir Felix Pole's son, John. No 5066 was an Old Oak Common locomotive for virtually its entire career, being withdrawn from there in September 1962. *J. A. Coiley*

Below:
Although recorded at Old Oak Common on 7 May 1959, No **5067** *St Fagans Castle* was actually allocated to Carmarthen at this time, having been reallocated from Bristol Bath Road in February of that year. Never fitted with a double chimney, No 5067 was transferred to Reading in May 1961, from where it was withdrawn in July of the following year. *Ian Allan Library*

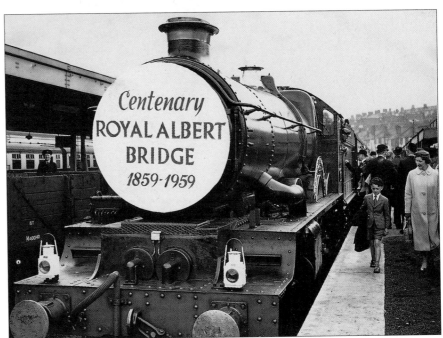

Right:
Originally named *Clifford Castle* when new, No **5071** became the first of 12 of the class to be renamed after Royal Air Force aircraft when it was renamed *Spitfire* in September 1940 following the success of the aircraft in the Battle of Britain. With steam to spare, the locomotive is pictured near Teignmouth on 19 July 1956 at the head of the down 'Cornishman'. Fitted with a double chimney in May 1959, No 5071 would end its days allocated to Bristol St Philips Marsh, from where it was withdrawn in October 1963. *R. C. Riley*

Below:
On 3 July 1957 No **5072** *Hurricane* heads westwards with the down 'Royal Duchy' at Newton Abbot. Originally named *Compton Castle*, the locomotive was renamed after one of the classic British single-seat fighters of World War 2 — the Hawker Hurricane — in November 1940. Allocated to Laira only in February 1957, the locomotive was transferred to Stafford Road in April 1958, where it remained, except for a month at Cardiff Canton in late 1960, until withdrawal in October 1962. *R. C. Riley*

Left:
On 24 July 1951, No **5073** *Blenheim* is pictured at Leominster with a service from Shrewsbury whilst on the adjacent platform Class 14xx No 1455 stands with a branch train from Kington. Passenger services over the line to Kington would survive for a further four years, being withdrawn on 7 February 1955. No 5073 had originally been named *Cranbrook Castle*, but was renamed after the Bristol Blenheim in January 1941. The locomotive was fitted with a double chimney in July 1959 and was withdrawn in February 1964. It was one of only three of the class built prewar to achieve a recorded mileage of less than one million miles. *R. C. Riley*

Above:
No **5074** *Hampden* had been a south Wales-based locomotive since moving to Cardiff Canton in August 1954, after which it spent time at Landore and Canton again before moving to Old Oak Common in January 1957. However, when recorded the next year, No 5074 was on Landore shed, having by then acquired a Hawksworth tender. It went back to South Wales in July 1960 at Landore and also worked out of Neath, Llanelly and Cardiff East Dock before withdrawal from Bristol St Philips Marsh in May 1964. Built in July 1938, No 5074 was originally named *Denbigh Castle*, but was renamed *Hampden* in January 1941. It was fitted with a double chimney in September 1961. *P. M. Alexander/Colour-Rail*

Above:
Renamed after the classic RAF Vickers-built bomber of World War 2, No **5075** *Wellington* was originally named *Devizes Castle* until October 1940. Seen here on 17 May 1948, the locomotive is pictured on the 7.25am Shrewsbury-Paddington service in the chalk cutting between Princes Risborough and Saunderton. Although it is now some five months after Nationalisation, the locomotive still lacks its BR numberplate and its tender still betrays its 'Big Four' origins. Allocated to Wolverhampton Stafford Road at the time, No 5075 would be subsequently allocated to Chester before heading to Laira. From Laira it would move to Exeter in July 1959 and thence, via Neath and Cardiff Canton, to its final shed, Bristol Bath Road, where it was based between July 1962 and its withdrawal two months later. *H. K. Harman*

Right:
It's December 1963 and Old Oak Common-allocated No **5076** *Gladiator* — named after the Gloster Gladiator bi-plane — awaits departure from Oxford with an up service for Paddington. The locomotive had been allocated to 81A since April and would be destined to spend just over a year based there before being transferred to Southall in June 1964, from where it was withdrawn three months later. Until January 1941, the locomotive had been named *Dryslwyn Castle. I. J. Hodson*

Left:
Two 'Castles' — No 7007 *Great Western* on the left and No **5077** *Fairey Battle* on the right — are seen at Paddington in May 1953. No 5077 was originally named *Eastnor Castle*, but was to be renamed after the aircraft in October 1940. Note, in particular, the special headboard carried by No 5077 as a tribute to the Coronation of HM Queen Elizabeth II. No 5077 was allocated to Taunton and in South Wales for much of its career, being finally transferred in June 1961 to Llanelly, from where it was withdrawn in July 1962. *W. J. Reynolds*

Centre left:
On 20 July 1956 No **5078** *Beaufort* catches the attention of holidaymakers at Teignmouth as it heads a service from Paignton to York. In the background can be seen Teignmouth's pier and, beyond that, the rocky promontory of Shaldon — popular destinations for many holidaymakers in the area. No 5078 was originally named *Lamphey Castle*, but acquired its new name in January 1941. Allocated at this time to Newton Abbot, No 5078 passed eventually to Neath in June 1961. In December 1961, the locomotive became the last of the class to be fitted with a double chimney, although the locomotive was to run with this modification for only a short time as it was withdrawn in November 1962. *R. C. Riley*

Lower left:
Recorded on 20 September 1955 at Westerleigh, No **5079** *Lysander* heads the down 'Cornishman'. No 5079 was originally named *Lydford Castle*, but was renamed after the Lysander — an aircraft used widely by the Royal Air Force during World War 2 for covert operations to Europe — in November 1940. Allocated to Newton Abbot when photographed, the locomotive was to remain there until final withdrawal in May 1960. *R. C. Riley*

Right:
In July 1962, in what must have been its last visit to its birthplace for repair, No **5080** *Defiant* stands alongside No 6905. A Cardiff Canton-allocated locomotive for many years, No 5080 was transferred to Llanelly in June 1961. Named originally *Ogmore Castle*, the locomotive was renamed after a two-seat fighter, the Boulton Paul Defiant, in January 1941. The locomotive was to survive, allocated to Llanelly, until withdrawal in April 1963. After withdrawal, it was eventually sold to Woodham Bros scrapyard at Barry, where it was to remain for nearly a decade until rescued, initially as a source of spare parts, by the Birmingham Railway Museum in August 1974. The locomotive has subsequently been restored to running order and is today displayed at Quainton Road.
J. W. Rainey

Above:
On 7 March 1955 No **5081** *Lockheed Hudson* heads past Norton Junction, just to the south of Worcester, shortly after departing from that city with an up express to Paddington. Originally named *Penrice Castle*, No 5081 acquired its new name — derived from the US-built medium bomber that served with the RAF during the war — in January 1941. It was the only one of the class to be renamed after a US-built type; all the other aircraft so honoured were British-built and it is curious that a relatively minor aircraft was commemorated when there were other more significant types, such as the Lancaster, Halifax and Stirling, that were not. Allocated to Worcester, No 5081 was reallocated to Cardiff Canton in September 1960 and then to Cardiff East Dock in August 1962. No 5081 would survive in service until October 1963.
T. E. Williams/Courtesy National Railway Museum

Left:
On 24 August 1957, No **5082** *Swordfish* heads northwards near Denham on the down 'Cambrian Coast Express'. Originally named *Powis Castle*, No 5082 was renamed in January 1941 after the Fairey Swordfish — an aircraft type, nicknamed the 'Stringbag', that had proved itself to be an effective weapon in the maritime war despite its antiquated appearance, achieving lasting fame in the campaign to sink the German battleship *Scharnhorst*. Allocated when photographed to Old Oak Common, it remained London-based until withdrawal in July 1962.
C. R. L. Coles/Rail Archive Stephenson

Below:
In 1949, No **5083** *Bath Abbey*, numerically the first of the 10 'Star' rebuilds of 1937-1940, heads an up service from Cheltenham at Wormwood Scrubs. Although the locomotive has, by this date, acquired a smokebox numberplate, it still lacks a shedplate. If it had possessed the latter, it would have recorded the fact that No 5083 at this date was allocated to Swindon. It was latterly allocated to Worcester, from where it was withdrawn in January 1959, the second of this batch of locomotives to succumb.
Ian Allan Library

Right:
With No 5023 *Brecon Castle* in the background, No **5084** *Reading Abbey* stands at Old Oak Common in light steam on 16 May 1957. This was the first one to emerge of the batch of 10 rebuilt from 'Star' class locomotives between April 1937 and November 1940. By May 1957, No 5084 was allocated to Old Oak Common and it remained there until withdrawal in July 1962. No 5084 was never fitted with a double chimney.
Ian Allan Library

Below:
On 10 May 1956 No **5085** *Evesham Abbey* makes a fine sight at Iver as it heads westwards with a down service to Bristol. Allocated by this stage to Bristol Bath Road, it would be transferred to Bristol St Philips Marsh in September 1960. Transferred again to Reading in August 1962 and thence via Neath (in October 1962) and Llanelly (February 1963) back to St Philips Marsh in March 1963, from where it was withdrawn in February the following year. No 5085 was never fitted with a double chimney.
Ian Allan Library

Upper left:
Recorded at Slough on 26 May 1953, No **5086** *Viscount Horne* heads a down service for Oxford, Worcester and Malvern. In December 1937, this was the third of the 10 members of the class to be reconstructed from 'Star' class 4-6-0s. The work in conversion included the welding of a frame extension to the cab, a rebuilt cab and the replacement of the No 1 boiler with a No 8. Although rebuilds, the GWR regarded, for accounting purposes, these 10 locomotives as brand-new, although crews regarded them as less successful than genuinely new examples, and there were undoubted failures, most notably from cracked frames. Allocated to Worcester for much of its career, No 5086 was one of the earliest casualties, being withdrawn in November 1958. *Ian Allan Library*

Centre left:
On 27 October 1956 No **5087** *Tintern Abbey* heads northwards with the down 'Cambrian Coast Express' near South Harefield platform. An Old Oak Common locomotive at the time, No 5087 would be transferred to Llanelly in December 1961, from where it was withdrawn in August 1963. When completed in November 1940, No 5087 was the last of the batch of 10 locomotives rebuilt from older 'Star' class 4-6-0s. *C. R. L. Coles/Rail Archive Stephenson*

Right:
Constructed notionally as a 'Star' rebuild in February 1939, Stafford Road-allocated No **5088** *Llanthony Abbey* had been fitted with a double chimney — in June 1958 — when recorded at Old Oak Common on 20 April 1961. Only three of this batch of 'Star' rebuilds were so treated. No 5088 was allocated to Stafford Road until it was withdrawn in September 1962. *M. Pope*

Right:
Approaching Widney Manor station at 6.38pm on 8 July 1958, No **5089** *Westminster Abbey* heads northbound with the 12.15pm Kingswear-Wolverhampton (Low Level) service. Note the reversed headboard: it was normal practice at that time for the board to be reversed during the summer season when the train operated in two parts. No 5089 was the penultimate of the 10 rebuilt locomotives in the late 1930s, being completed in October 1939. In July 1958, the locomotive had only recently been transferred to Stafford Road; it was to remain there until a final transfer saw it migrate across Wolverhampton, to Oxley, in September 1963, from where it was withdrawn in November the following year. *M. Mensing*

Left:
In the autumn of its career, No **5090** *Neath Abbey* waits at Bristol Temple Meads with a parcels train. Displaying its 81A shedplate, to which No 5090 was transferred in October 1960, the locomotive was destined to survive in service based at Old Oak Common until May 1962. *George Heiron*

Right:
No **5091** *Cleeve Abbey* heads southeastwards near Wellington, in Shropshire, with an up semi-fast service on 6 August 1956. Allocated to Chester, No 5091 passed to Exeter in July 1957, to Carmarthen in September 1957, to Landore in June 1958, to Llanelly in June 1961, to Cardiff Canton in September 1961, and to Cardiff East Dock in August 1962 when Canton's remaining steam allocation was transferred to permit the rebuilding of the shed as a diesel depot. It then moved to Worcester in April 1964 and finally to Tyseley in June 1964. No 5091 was to be withdrawn four months later. *Brian Morrison*

Above left:
On 20 September 1955 No **5092** *Tresco Abbey* makes a fine sight as its storms through Chipping Sodbury with an up service from Fishguard. Although numerically the last of the 10 'Castle' class locomotive rebuilt from 'Star' class 4-6-0s between 1937 and 1940, No 5092 was actually completed relatively early in the programme, in April 1938. Fitted with a double chimney in October 1961, the locomotive was withdrawn in July 1963 from Cardiff East Dock, to where it had been transferred the previous August. *R. C. Riley*

Left:
A passing couple glance to their right as No **5093** *Upton Castle* heads east towards Dawlish with the up 'Torbay Express' on 19 July 1956. Allocated to Landore when first built in June 1939, No 5083 had been reallocated to Old Oak Common by the time it was recorded here. It was to remain allocated to 81A for the rest of its working life, being withdrawn from there in September 1963. *R. C. Riley*

Above:
On 19 October 1957 No **5094** *Tretower Castle*, looking in excellent condition externally, heads past West London Sidings with the 2.15pm service from Paddington to Gloucester. Allocated at this time to Gloucester, the locomotive was transferred to Bristol Bath Road in August 1960, following the fitting of a double chimney in the previous June, and thence to Bristol St Philips Marsh the following month. No 5094 was to survive in service until September 1962. *R. C. Riley*

Left:
Standing under the fine overall roof at Paddington station on 24 August 1957, No **5095** *Barbury Castle* has just arrived in London with the 8am service from Neyland, although the locomotive was changed at Cardiff. In the background a superb vintage Rolls Royce is also visible. No 5095 was at this time allocated to Cardiff Canton but would be transferred to Shrewsbury in September 1960. Fitted with a double-chimney in November 1958, No 5095 survived until withdrawal in August 1962. *D. C. Ovenden*

Centre left:
In 1962, Cardiff Canton-allocated No **5096** *Bridgwater Castle* heads eastbound at Shrivenham with an eastbound express for Paddington. A Bristol-based locomotive for much of its career, it spent 30 months allocated to Cardiff Canton or East Dock, before a final transfer to Worcester in April 1964. The locomotive was withdrawn two months later. *T. E. Williams/Courtesy National Railway Museum*

Right:
Recorded at Cardiff Canton, its home shed, on 25 February 1962, No **5097** *Sarum Castle* had only recently — in July 1961 — been fitted with a double chimney and had migrated to Canton two months later. Its sojourn there was, however, shortlived; with Canton's closure to steam in August 1962, the locomotive moved to Cardiff East Dock, from where it was withdrawn in March 1963. *R. J. Henly*

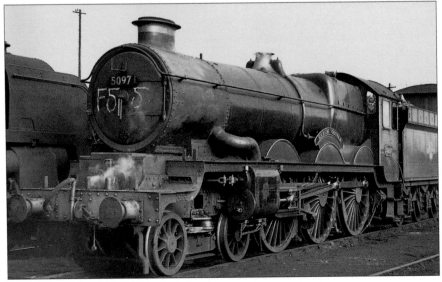

Above:
No **5098** *Clifford Castle*, standing outside Laira shed, where it was allocated, on 30 April 1961, was the first member of the class to be completed after the cessation of hostilities in 1945, emerging from Swindon Works in May 1946. Fitted with a double chimney in January 1959, No 5098 was reallocated to Newton Abbot in January 1962 and then, via Carmarthen, Llanelly and Old Oak Common, to Reading in April 1964. Its sojourn in the Thames Valley was, however, destined to be relatively short as the locomotive was withdrawn two months later. *R. C. Riley*

Below:
Recorded at Wantage Road in September 1961 at the head of the up 'Red Dragon', No **5099** *Compton Castle* was one of four of the class to be completed during May 1946. At this date the locomotive was based at Cardiff Canton. However, it was to be transferred to Worcester in February 1962 and again to Gloucester Horton Road seven months later. Never fitted with a double chimney, No 5099 was finally withdrawn from Gloucester in February 1963. *T. E. Williams/Courtesy National Railway Museum*

Above:
Heading westbound with the down 'Torbay Express'
No **7000** *Viscount Portal* has just passed through Whiteball
Tunnel on 4 September 1954 and the crew will be looking
forward to the long descent to Exeter now that the summit,
at Whiteball Siding signalbox, has been reached. Allocated
to Newton Abbot from new, No 7000 was transferred to
Cardiff Canton between May and August 1957, before
returning to 83A. From Newton Abbot it eventually passed
to Gloucester in June 1959 and then to Worcester in
February 1963, from where it was withdrawn in December
the same year. The signalbox illustrated here was to be
destroyed by fire in 1955, when the duty signalman had a
problem refilling an oil lamp. Having notified the next box
of his problems, the signalman made his way, wearing
carpet slippers, to an adjacent farm in the dark to raise the
alarm. The box was subsequently rebuilt. *R. C. Riley*

Left:
Pictured at Whiteball Siding signalbox
on 21 July 1956, No **7001** *Sir James
Milne* is providing the motive power
for the 8.45am service from Liverpool
to Penzance. The consist of 12
carriages was formed of LMR stock.
No 7001 was built in May 1946 and
was fitted with a double chimney in
September 1960. Allocated to Old
Oak Common for much of its career,
it was transferred to Stafford Road in
September 1961 and then to Oxley in
August 1963, the month before its
withdrawal. No 7001 had originally
been named *Denbigh Castle* but was
renamed after the last chairman of the
GWR in February 1948. *R. C. Riley*

Right:
Pictured at Swansea High Street on
4 August 1951, No **7002** *Devizes
Castle* is just departing with the
3.45pm service from Paddington to
Fishguard. The 'Castle' had replaced
'Hall' No 5939 *Tangley Hall*, which
had brought the service into Swansea
from the east, and would be piloted by
the 0-6-0PT as far as Laughor, which
was normal practice for westbound
services out of Swansea. A Landore-
allocated locomotive, No 7002 had
inherited its name from No 5075
when built in June 1946. The
locomotive subsequently passed to
Carmarthen and then back to Landore
for a period between June 1958 and
December 1959, when a final transfer
took it to Worcester. Fitted with a
double chimney in July 1961,
withdrawal was to come in March
1964. *R. C. Riley*

Centre right: Pictured in ex-Works
condition at Swindon on 15 June
1952, No **7003** *Elmley Castle* was
exactly six years old. Built in June
1946, it was at this time allocated to
Landore, where it would remain until
transferred to Bristol Bath Road in
December 1958. In July 1960, shortly
after it was fitted with a double
chimney, it was reallocated to
Gloucester Horton Road, where it
remained (except for a brief period
between April and June 1964) until
withdrawal in August 1964.
R. C. Riley

Lower right:
No **7004** *Eastnor Castle* is pictured at
Cullompton during 1955 whilst at the
head of the down 'Torbay Express'.
An Old Oak Common-allocated
locomotive at this time, No 7004
would be fitted with a double
chimney in February 1958 before
being transferred to Worcester in July
1960. A further transfer saw the
locomotive move to Reading in
September 1963, from where it was
withdrawn in January 1964. *Ian Allan
Library*

Left:
With its 85A Worcester shedplate clearly visible, No **7005** *Sir Edward Elgar* stands outside Cardiff Canton on 5 January 1962. Named originally *Lamphey Castle*, No 7005 had been renamed after the famous composer in August 1957 to mark the centenary of his birth. No 7005 was to survive in service until September 1964. *R. J. Henly*

Below left:
No **7006** *Lydford Castle* gleams in the summer sun as it heads westwards whilst picking up water at Goring troughs with the down 4.55pm service from Paddington to Cheltenham on 10 June 1950. Appropriately allocated to Gloucester Horton Road at the time, April 1958 would see the locomotive transferred to Laira. Fitted with a double chimney in June 1960, the locomotive returned briefly to Gloucester between July and September that year before a transfer to Worcester. A final reallocation in March 1962 to Old Oak Common followed, from where the locomotive was withdrawn in December 1963. *J. F. Russell-Smith/Courtesy National Railway Museum*

Above:
With the appropriately Gothic lettering of its headboard proclaiming the train to be the 'Cathedrals Express', No **7007** *Great Western* awaits departure with the down service to Worcester and Hereford. Built in July 1946, No 7007 was the last of the class to be completed before Nationalisation of the railways in 1948 and was originally named *Ogmore Castle*. It received its new name, as a tribute to the erstwhile GWR, in January 1948 — note the GWR coat of arms on the splasher beneath the nameplate. It was allocated to Wolverhampton Stafford Road when new, moving quickly on to Old Oak Common and then to Worcester in February 1950 from where it was withdrawn in February 1963. Although the photograph is undated, it was certainly taken before June 1961 when the locomotive was fitted with a double chimney. *N. E. Preedy*

Right:
Literally in the evening of its career — it was 8.25pm on 5 June 1964 — No **7008** *Swansea Castle* of Old Oak Common, which had been fitted with a double chimney in June 1959, departs from Southall with the Fridays-only postal vans service from Southall to Wrexham. Completed in May 1948, No 7008 was the first of the class to be completed under BR ownership. The locomotive was destined to have barely another three months in service, being withdrawn from service, still allocated to 81A, in September of the same year. *S. E. Teasdale*

Above:
Heading westwards at Southall on 10 August 1957, Landore-allocated No **7009** *Athelney Castle* was making light work of the five-coach 2.20pm Paddington-Shrewsbury via Swindon parcels service. Reallocated to Carmarthen in September 1960 and to Old Oak Common the following July, No 7009 spent brief periods, from February to October 1962 at Worcester and until December at Gloucester, before returning to 81A from where the locomotive was withdrawn in March 1963. *R. C. Riley*

Left:
Built in June 1948, No **7010** *Avondale Castle* was barely eight years old when recorded in ex-Works condition at Swindon on 6 May 1956 prior to returning to its home shed at Old Oak Common. Fitted with a double chimney in November 1960, No 7010 would remain at 81A until January 1964 when a move would see it transferred to Reading. However, its sojourn in Berkshire was destined to be short: it was withdrawn two months later. *P. H. Wells*

Right:

On 27 June 1962 Worcester-allocated No **7011** *Banbury Castle* departs from Hereford with an up service to Paddington. No 7011 would remain at Worcester until transferred to Reading in September 1962. After a further brief spell at Worcester, between January and June 1964, the locomotive ended its career at Oxley, being withdrawn in February 1965. *Derek Cross*

Below:

No **7012** *Barry Castle* leaves Wednesbury Tunnel on 13 June 1964 with the 10.50am service from Wolverhampton to Ramsgate and Margate. By this date No 7012 was in the autumn of its career; it would be withdrawn from Wolverhampton Oxley shed five months later, shortly after control of the shed had passed from the Western to the London Midland Region. No 7012 was never fitted with double chimney. *Paul Riley*

Above:
Although purporting to be postwar-built No **7013** *Bristol Castle*, this is in fact the original No 4082 *Windsor Castle* recorded at Old Oak Common on 31 September 1958. The original No 4082 had been driven by HRH the Duke of York — the future King George VI — during a visit to Swindon on 28 April 1924 and was therefore selected as the locomotive to haul the Royal funeral train from Paddington to Windsor. Unfortunately, however, when the King died suddenly in 1952, No 4082 was at Worcester Shed awaiting repair and was not available to work the train. It was, as a result, decided to swap identities with No 7013 but, given the detail differences between the two locomotives, the deception was noted and therefore the two locomotives never resumed their original identities. No 7013 was withdrawn from Tyseley in February 1965. *R. C. Riley*

Above:
Recorded in the twilight of its career, No **7014** *Caerhays Castle* heads southbound in April 1963 down Hatton Bank with a service from Wolverhampton to Margate. The locomotive had been transferred to Stafford Road in the previous July and would remain at 84A until reallocated to Oxley in September 1963 and then to Tyseley in June 1964, from where it was withdrawn during the following February. No 7014 had been fitted with a double chimney in February 1959. *Ian Allan Library*

Right:
Named after Collett's mentor and immediate predecessor as CME of the GWR, No **7017** *G. J. Churchward* was constructed at Swindon Works in August 1948. It is pictured at its home shed, Old Oak Common, looking in superb external condition on 29 August 1959. Never fitted with a double chimney, it was to remain allocated to 81A until final withdrawal in February 1963. *R. C. Riley*

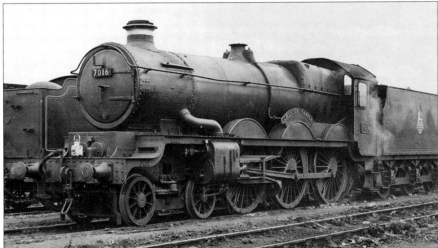

Left:
No **7016** *Chester Castle* is recorded early in its career when allocated to Cardiff Canton shed. Constructed in August 1948, No 7016 was subsequently to be allocated to Landore before passing to Carmarthen in September 1959. After a brief sojourn at Llanelly between July and September 1961, a further transfer took it back to Canton. Its last transfer occurred in August 1962, when it moved to Cardiff East Dock, but its time at this new shed was limited as it was withdrawn three months later.
Ian Allan Library

Above:

With the portal of Middle Hill Tunnel in the distance, No **7018** *Drysllwyn Castle* rushes through Box station with the down 'Bristolian' on 6 May 1958. In 1956 No 7018 had been the locomotive upon which an experimental double chimney with double blast pipe was tested. The success of the trials resulted in the first double chimney proper being fitted to No 4090; No 7018 was itself fitted with a new double chimney in May 1958, shortly after the date of this photograph. No 7018 was allocated to Bristol Bath Road at the time; it was transferred to St Philips Marsh in September 1960 and to Old Oak Common in October 1961. No 7018 was finally withdrawn in September 1963. *Ivo Peters*

Left:

With less than a year to survive until withdrawal, No **7019** *Fowey Castle* appears in reasonable external condition as recorded at Swindon shed on 3 May 1964. Fitted with a double chimney in August 1958, No 7019 was based by this date at Wolverhampton Oxley, having been transferred there in September 1963. One of a handful of the class to survive into 1965, No 7019 was to be withdrawn in February of that year. *N. E. Preedy*

Above:
On 13 June 1957 No **7020** *Gloucester Castle* arrives at Birmingham (Snow Hill) with the 2.35pm service from Birkenhead to Paddington. At this date the locomotive still retained its single chimney; a double chimney was not to be fitted until February 1961. When photographed, No 7020 had recently been allocated to Old Oak Common from Cardiff Canton. Its final shed, before withdrawal in September 1964 was Southall. *M. Mensing*

Right:
Pictured at Old Oak Common East signalbox on 29 August 1959, No **7021** *Haverfordwest Castle* heads the down 'Capitals United Express' westwards. Transferred to Landore only in the previous month, No 7021, which was to be fitted with a double chimney in November 1961, moved to Llanelly in June 1961 and then to Old Oak Common in December the same year. No 7021 was withdrawn in September 1963. *R. C. Riley*

Left:
On 9 May 1964, No **7022** *Hereford Castle* — with a non-standard smokebox numberplate — gets some attention outside Swindon shed. Alongside is an interloper in the guise of ex-LMS Stanier Pacific No 46251 *City of Nottingham.* As is evident from the shedplate, No 7022 was allocated to 85A, although this was only a recent move to Worcester, which had taken place two months earlier. No 7022 would remain allocated to Worcester until October 1964, when a final move saw it transferred to Gloucester, from where it was withdrawn in June 1965 — one of the few of the class to survive into that year. *P. H. Wells*

Above:
Recorded at Worcester Shed on 19 August 1962, this view of No **7023** *Penrice Castle* shows to good effect the double chimney fitted to the locomotive in May 1958. No 7023 had been allocated to Cardiff Canton until August 1960, when it was transferred to Worcester, where it would remain until reallocated to Oxley in June 1964. The locomotive was withdrawn in February 1965. *R. C. Riley*

Right:
With the town's 1790-built parish church as a backdrop, No **7025** *Sudeley Castle* passes through Wellington, Shropshire, with the up 'Cambrian Coast Express' in 1961. On the right of the photograph can be seen the water tower of the adjacent engine shed; this opened in 1876 and was provided with a turntable until the 1940s. Coded 84H by British Railways, the shed was to close on 10 August 1964. No 7025 had been transferred to Shrewsbury in August 1960 and passed to Worcester in September 1962, where it was to remain exactly two years until withdrawal in September 1964. *M. Pope*

Above:
No **7024** *Powis Castle*, constructed in June 1949, was delivered new to Old Oak Common. It remained based in London until transferred to Wolverhampton Stafford Road in September 1961. After exactly two years at 84A, it was transferred to the other Wolverhampton shed, Oxley, prior to being withdrawn in February 1965. It was fitted with a double chimney in March 1959 and is seen here soon after, still in sparkling condition, looking down from the cutting at Chipping Sodbury. *P. M. Alexander/ Colour-Rail*

Above:

On 4 April 1953 No **7026** *Tenby Castle* arrives at Birmingham (Snow Hill) with the 11.43am service from Birkenhead to Paddington. A Wolverhampton Stafford Road locomotive at this date, No 7026 would be transferred to Gloucester in September 1962 before returning to Stafford Road two months later. Following a further transfer to Oxley, in September 1963, the locomotive was withdrawn from Tyseley, where it had been reallocated in June 1964, in October 1964. No 7026 was one of a number of the final batch of 'Castles' that were never fitted with a double chimney. *R. J. Green*

Left:

One of eight members of the class to survive, No **7027** *Thornbury Castle* was originally built at Swindon in August 1949. For much of its career, No 7027 was allocated to Old Oak Common, but was transferred to Worcester in May 1960 and thence to Reading in August 1963. Following withdrawal in December 1963, the locomotive was sold to Woodham Bros at Barry. Arriving at Barry in June 1964, No 7027 would be rescued for preservation by the Birmingham Railway Museum in August 1972. *Ian Allan Library*

Above:

Lacking a shedplate, but with the ex-GWR code 'LDR' — for Landore — painted behind the buffer beam, No **7028** *Cadbury Castle*, built in May 1950, was almost brand-new when recorded here. Allocated to South Wales throughout its career, No 7028 was subsequently allocated to Carmarthen, Landore again and finally, from June 1961 to Llanelly. In October the same year, No 7028 was fitted with a double chimney and was to be withdrawn in December 1963.
Ian Allan Library

Right:

One of only a handful of 'Castle' class locomotives to survive into 1965, No **7029** *Clun Castle* was finally withdrawn in December of that year, Some six months earlier, on 28 June, the locomotive was recorded at Horton Road shed in Gloucester, where it been allocated the previous October from Old Oak Common. Fitted with a double chimney in October 1959, No 7029 was to be preserved after withdrawal, being based at the Birmingham Railway Museum at Tyseley. A regular performer since the return to steam in the early 1970s, No 7029 has now been in preservation for almost twice as long as it was in main line service and is still based at Tyseley.
N. E. Preedy

Left:
Pictured at Slough on 26 May 1953, No **7030** *Cranbrook Castle* was not yet three years old when recorded at the head of an up service from Torquay. Allocated to Old Oak Common throughout its career, No 7030 was fitted with a double chimney in July 1959. It was withdrawn from service in February 1963. *Ian Allan Library*

Above:
Laira-based No **7031** *Cromwell's Castle* is seen on Dainton Bank in 1956 with a service from Paddington to Plymouth. The locomotive spent several years based at Plymouth before being transferred to Swindon in September 1959 and Worcester in March 1962, from where it was withdrawn in July 1963. After a period in storage, No 7031 was cut-up at Cashmores in June 1964. *Ian Allan Library*

Right:
In June 1957 No **7032** *Denbigh Castle* rushes through Wednesbury Central station with the up 'Cambrian Coast Express'. Built in June 1950, No 7032 was to be fitted with a double chimney in September 1960. The locomotives was to be allocated to Old Oak Common for its entire working career, being withdrawn in September 1964 having completed a total of 666,374 miles in service by 28 December 1963 when recording of mileages ceased. *Ian Allan Library*

Above:
Old Oak Common-allocated No **7033** *Hartlebury Castle* had only recently been fitted with a double chimney when recorded passing Widney Manor station on Sunday 31 July 1960 at the head of the 1.10pm service from Paddington to Wolverhampton (Low Level). Constructed in July 1950, No 7033 was to remain an Old Oak Common locomotive throughout its 13-year career, being withdrawn in January 1963. *M. Mensing*

With the dramatic lines of Southall gas works in the background, a careworn No **7034** *Ince Castle* — fitted with a double-chimney in December 1959 — heads eastwards with an up freight train at 12.50pm on 30 December 1964. Allocated to Gloucester in December 1964, No 7034 was to remain based there until June 1965 when it was withdrawn, one of the last of the class to remain in service. *S. E. Teasdale*

Below:
Heading westwards at Challow on 16 August 1960, No **7035** *Ogmore Castle* is pictured at the head of the down 'Cheltenham Spa Express'. Built in August 1950, No 7035 had been fitted with a double chimney in January 1960 and reallocated to Gloucester Horton Road two months later. From Gloucester, No 7035 was transferred to Oxford in November 1962 and finally to Old Oak Common in February 1963, from where it was withdrawn in June 1964. *T. E. Williams/Courtesy National Railway Museum*

Above:

The penultimate 'Castle' numerically, No **7036** *Taunton Castle*, was completed in August 1950 and fitted with a double chimney in August 1959. It is seen in this modified condition heading westwards under Westbourne Bridge with the down 4.10pm service to Birkenhead on 27 August 1960. At this time the locomotive was allocated to Old Oak Common as it was, except for a brief period between July and September 1962 when it was based at Stafford Road, until withdrawal in September 1963. *R. C. Riley*

Right:

The last 'Castle' constructed, No **7037** *Swindon,* was built at Swindon in August 1950, the last express locomotive to be constructed to an ex-GWR design. Pictured, appropriately, at Swindon Junction on 12 January 1953, the locomotive is providing the motive power for the down Whitland milk empties. Never fitted with a double chimney, No 7037 was allocated to Worcester from September to November 1950, but then, again appropriately, spent most of its career to Swindon. The only exceptions were a month in 1959 when it was based at Cardiff Canton and immediately before its withdrawal in March 1963, when it was allocated to Old Oak Common. When withdrawn, No 7037 had achieved the lowest recorded mileage of any member of the class — some 519,885 miles. *R. C. Riley*

Left:
On withdrawal in May 1960, No 4073 *Caerphilly Castle* was stored for seven months at Swindon Works before being restored for display at the Science Museum in London. On 2 June 1961, in the company of diesel shunter No D4004, No 4073 made its final appearance, in superb condition, at Paddington before the move from Park Royal to South Kensington by road. The locomotive had been propelled into Paddington by the diesel locomotive prior to presentation to Sir David Follett, the Director of the Science Museum. *R. C. Riley*

Caerphilly Castle's Finale

Left:
The passengers on board RT2002 can't have expected to see this sight when heading from Kensington to Harlesden on 4 June 1961. Equally bemused in Park Royal Road is the family on the extreme right. The move from Park Royal to South Kensington was accomplished using two tractor/trailer units; fortunately, traffic was considerably lighter in the early 1960s. *R. C. Riley*

Right:
Under the wary eye of a policeman, No 4073 is pictured on Westbourne Grove; curiously, the locomotive's move was not the main feature at the Odeon! *R. C. Riley*

Right:
With a crowd of onlookers watching its stately progress, the Pickfords' ensemble is recorded in Kensington Church Street. *R. C. Riley*

Below:
The two tractor/trailer sets are the centre of attraction in All Saints Road. Note the lack of traffic, parked cars and road markings; how times have changed! No 4073 was the centrepiece of the transport display at the Science Museum for some 40 years until it was decided to reorder the display galleries. The reverse procedure saw the locomotive removed from the Museum, again by road, and transferred to the National Railway Museum at York. *R. C. Riley*

Epilogue

No 7029 was used by the Western Region to mark the final main line steam services out of Paddington on two occasions: on 11 June 1965 it powered the last scheduled steam-hauled service over the cut-off route to Banbury and on 27 November 1965 it hauled the last official steam working from Paddington. On 1 January 1966 it hauled its (and the class's) final service, the 5pm from Gloucester to Cheltenham, and, later that same month, was to be privately preserved. Based at Tyseley, the future Birmingham Railway Museum, the locomotive continued to see limited use on freight trains between Birmingham and Banbury despite being in private ownership. The concluding view in this book, taken in July 1966, sees No 7029 powering one of these freights — a coal train for the Greaves Cement Siding — at Harbury Tunnel. *J. R. P. Hunt*